MOTIVATIONAL LEVERAGE

A New Approach to Managing People

MOTIVATIONAL LEVERAGE

A New Approach to Managing People

William Exton, Jr.

PARKER PUBLISHING COMPANY, INC. West Nyack, N.Y.

Library of Congress Cataloging in Publication Data

Exton, William.
  Motivational leverage.

  1. Psychology, Industrial. 2. Motivation (Psy-
chology) I. Title.
HF5548.8.E9 1975   658.3   74-13921
ISBN 0-13-604082-9

This book is inevitably dedicated to William Exton, III, the most effective exerciser of Motivational Leverage within the experience of the author; and who has already developed his irresistible expertise before reaching the age of eight.

HOW THIS BOOK
WILL BENEFIT YOU

This book is about new approaches to the purposeful, constructive and effective motivating of people for specific purposes. We call these new and systematic approaches "Motivational Leverage."

Most of the motivating that goes on in the world is called persuading, encouraging, leading, negotiating, tempting, inducing, bargaining, influencing, selling, convincing, cajoling, urging, example-setting, promising, etc. This book tells about the principles and the new techniques that underlie the effective and successful application of Motivational Leverage to all such widespread, basic, and essential forms of motivating as these, whether in everyday situations or in the most important, critical emergencies.

Everyone needs to use these ways of dealing with other people almost all the time, for purposes that vary from the incidental to the very serious, and everyone is happy and pleased when they produce the desired and hoped for results; and everyone is unhappy and disappointed when they do not. This book can help *you* to be successful in influencing people through the application of this new System of Motivational Leverage.

The greatest advantage you can have in getting what you want out of life is the ability to influence others—and that is what this book is all about.

Scientists (psychologists, sociologists, psychiatrists, an-

5

thropologists and others) have explored many aspects of motivation
and its mechanisms; and what they have to say is important. But
they do not all agree; and anyhow it is not very easy to know how to
apply all they write about to the reality of one's own life.

On the other hand, more practical people (such as personnel
experts, sales managers, marketers, advertising people and many
successful executives) have also written about motivation, and their
wisdom also has great value. But it is often very specialized and
scattered, and it is usually very personal in that most of it relates
only to each one's own experience and interests.

This book combines the basic solidity of generally acceptable
scientific knowledge with down-to-earth practicality, born of the
author's many years of experience. The underlying, vital principles
are explained in non-scientific language and they are then illustrated
with realistic examples—most of them with dialogue that shows
clearly the kind of talk that produces the desired results. Every effort
has been made to keep everything as clear and as simple as the
subject will allow.

This book also reduces the great and complex mass of available
information about motivation to a simple, basic Motivational Leverage System, originated by the author. This *System* is easy to understand and to apply, and this book is designed to help you understand
it and to apply it successfully.

In Chapter 1 you will learn how to persuade other people to act
for your benefit. You will discover how to "figure the
Potentials"—what you can expect to be able to accomplish through
motivation. You will also be introduced to Motivational Leverage,
and to the Motivational Leverage System, and to such important
elements of the System as your *Standing,* and your *Advantage*—and
how to develop and apply these through your own behavior to
maximize your Motivational Leverage to produce the results you
want.

Chapter 2 helps you to understand people better: their hidden
reasons for acting as they do, and "what makes them tick." And in
Chapters 3 and 4 you will find out about the five *big, basic*
motivators, and how you can secure powerful Motivational Leverage by using these to improve your *Advantage.*

Chapters 5 and 6 tell you how to make and use a *Target Plan* to
gain what you want by applying Motivational Leverage to the cor-

rectly chosen *Target Individual*—and right there you will find the key to the success of the Motivational Leverage System. Chapters 7 and 8 explain how to win the support of others; how to get agreement; how to handle problems of disagreement; how to set the winning strategies and tactics that can help you to get ahead in the direction you choose; and more.

Chapter 9 shows you how you can apply the book's Motivational Leverage System even in rather difficult situations. Chapter 10 helps you to apply the System in competition, and tells how to use the System regularly, not only to move up in the world, but even as you reach the top. Also, this book tells you how to use the Motivational Leverage System to help others—and more.

Whenever one person influences another to make a decision or to perform an action or to have an attitude, certain processes are at work. These processes are fundamental. If we understand these processes, we are half-way to using them effectively. The other half is technique—how *well* we use them. We need both halves—we need to understand the processes and also how to put them to work.

This book is particularly planned both to help people understand the necessary processes of motivation, and also to learn the techniques for motivating others. The organization of the book follows a logical, simple development of ideas that flow naturally from principle to technique to application. Many realistic examples are given to illustrate the applications of the processes of Motivational Leverage to specific, practical situations, and to show how techniques make the processes effective.

You will find included, examples covering almost every kind of situation. As you go along, you should try to think of situations in your own experience that are similar to the examples given in this book. In this way you can gain an excellent understanding of the ways in which the Motivational Leverage System applies in real life, and how the techniques can be made to fit actual conditions to bring about your own success in motivating others.

A word of caution, however. Some people, unfortunately, use their ability to motivate others to the others' detriment: they take advantage of other people, dominate them, cheat them, deceive them. This is far different from motivating people for their own good; and also a far cry from the perfectly legitimate purpose of motivating them to act for one's own benefit, but without detriment to themselves, as by invoking their helpfulness. This book has been written for those interested in learning the fair, decent, constructive and legitimate applications of Motivational Leverage, which can be enormously helpful when properly directed.

Reading it in this spirit, you will surely find this book valuable to you in gaining insight, knowledge, understanding and "know-how" that can help you greatly in the successful application of Motivational Leverage.

William Exton, Jr.

CONTENTS

1

INTRODUCING
MOTIVATIONAL LEVERAGE:
NEW APPROACHES FOR
MANAGING PEOPLE

Some people just seem to have what it takes to get other people to do what they want. People like that have Motivational Leverage. Others have a bad time.

There are all sorts of reasons for such big, important differences and most people who understand those reasons and those differences can begin to do something useful about them. They can do something useful and effective about building Motivational Leverage for themselves.

Let us begin by looking at a lucky fellow who already has all kinds of potent Motivational Leverage going for him.

1. HOW YOU CAN BEGIN TO USE MOTIVATIONAL LEVERAGE IN GETTING OTHER PEOPLE TO HELP YOU TO REACH YOUR GOALS

Little Willie Burns is just two weeks old. He is hungry, and so he is crying. But Little Willie is lucky. There are a lot of people who really care about him—people who do not want him to be hungry. So Little Willie cries—and gets himself fed. And likewise, when Little Willie is wet, he also cries—and gets himself changed.

Little Willie has a lot of Motivational Leverage—but only because people *want* to do things for him—to help him—feed him —change him—take care of him—give him what he needs and wants.

Other people are really only waiting for a cue—a signal—some indication that Little Willie needs or wants some attention. Their desire to do for him is already there—it only waits for its cue (and sometimes it even works in anticipation, before the cue).

Recognizing Those Who Are Already Favorable to You

All the people that leap into action when Little Willie cries are already motivated. They are motivated by love, duty, instinct, cultural patterns, training, and all the other powerful factors that make mothers, fathers, grandparents and relatives—even nurses and maids, and even some friends and neighbors—find satisfaction in cuddling Little Willie and ministering to him and making or keeping him happy.

So, Little Willie is lucky. He doesn't have to motivate the people around him. They are already motivated. All he has to do is give out signals. And as Willie grows up, he will learn a lot about how to manipulate his mother, his father, his aunts and uncles, his grandparents—and maybe even his brothers and sisters, and some of his classmates and friends. He will learn the basic lesson—it is easier to motivate people to do what you want them to when they are already favorable to you.

A few blocks away from Little Willie there is another baby, in another kind of home. The people around him were troubled and unhappy and quarreling before he came, and now it is worse. He was not wanted, he is not loved, and he does not have very much going for him. There is very little motivation around him to take care of this unfortunate child. When he cries, most of those nearby take it as an annoyance and a nuisance, rather than as a signal to rush in with loving, tender care. If he cries long enough, maybe somebody will do something, but this poor little fellow has very little power to motivate those around him. He often signals in vain.

When Little Willie grows up and approaches manhood, he will, of course, begin to take an interest in girls. After a while there will be a special girl—maybe even a *very* special girl, and Willie will spend a lot of time thinking about how he'd like her to behave toward him. And he will make a variety of efforts to get her to behave that way—and he may have some success—but probably not all he wants—not enough to satisfy him.

Willie tries to *motivate* the young lady. If she is already somewhat motivated, he can make quite a lot of progress; but if she isn't motivated that way, it may be very slow going for Willie.

If Willie is somewhat frustrated then, he may indulge in fantasies, imagining himself as a sultan or a caliph or a pasha, or some other kind of oriental potentate, with a large harem of beautiful women, and with absolute power over them. They are all very anxious to please him because, if they fail, he can have them severely punished or thrown to the crocodiles or what have you. Such threats of severely unpleasant penalties can have a potent motivating effect it seems, and the ladies in Willie's dreams of harem life tend to be extremely cooperative and even vie for his favor.

Recognizing That You Need People to Be Favorable to You

When Willie is a few years older he will go to work, and then, no matter what sort of job he has, he will find the same old problem: not everyone is motivated to do just as Willie would like them to do. (Life is no longer as it was when Willie was a lucky, lucky baby.)

Willie is a salesman: not every prospect will buy; and some of them give him a hard time. Even those who buy are often bothersome: they complain about prices, and deliveries, and defects; they speak favorably of the competition; they create credit problems; they expect special treatment; they cause extra trouble, and many difficulties; and they take up lots of time, etc. Clearly, they are not motivated to make life prosperous and happy for Willie the salesman.

Willie is in an office: his supervisor is slow to recognize Willie's special merits; does not put him in the choice spots; and misses the chances to promote Willie, or to raise his pay. Some of his fellow workers are less than friendly; even unfriendly. The senior people around him tend to be stand-offish and cliquey; and at the same time some of the youngsters seem less than respectful.

Clearly, these people are not motivated to make life more pleasant and more successful for Willie.

And so it goes, wherever Willie goes to work; in factory or institution, government or private industry; in distribution or production; in small or large business; etc. Willie very seldom finds people who are really motivated to help *him*. No wonder he often thinks back to his childhood home, when at least a few people could be counted on to indulge him because they *were* motivated to please him—to help him get what he wanted (or, at least, some of what he wanted).

How to Move Toward More Favorable Attitudes in Others

No wonder Willie is often displeased, annoyed, frustrated. His discontent, his unhappiness, can almost always be traced to someone else's behavior: what someone else is doing or not doing. How greatly he wishes they would behave or act in whatever manner would open the way to what he wants! How, then, he wonders, can he motivate them to do as he wishes?

That is a good question. A *very* good question. And the men or women who can find answers to this question can lead an entirely different kind of life from those who cannot. They are not stopped at the first barrier; new horizons of opportunity and reward open up for them. They find ways to remove obstacles that hold others back; they do not let people stand arbitrarily in their way. They exert more control over their own lives; they can lead fuller lives; they find fewer frustrations and more satisfactions.

How Motivational Leverage Helps to Get the Results You Want

So, it would seem, the ability to apply Motivational Leverage can be a very useful attribute indeed. Most of us have more of this ability than we realize, and probably far more of it than we are using. We *can* motivate others far more effectively than we do now. We need to learn how to use the favorable attitudes of others, and how to make others' attitudes toward us more favorable.

But a favorable attitude alone is not enough. For people to be motivated to assist us in specific ways, they must have an attitude that is favorable to our specific goals. If you want your boss to promote you, it is not enough for him to be favorable to you as a luncheon companion or a golf partner (though such attitudes can help).

Developing the Priceless Ability to Influence Others Favorably

With most bosses, you would need to create an attitude that is specifically favorable toward you as a candidate for promotion to the position you want. The ability to foster such focussed attitudes—to motivate people favorably for specific purposes—*can* be developed. But you can learn how to do this far better if you understand the psychological and emotional and social principles that underlie the processes by which people condition their feelings and initiate their actions about others.

2. HOW TO USE MOTIVATIONAL LEVERAGE TO PERSUADE OTHER PEOPLE TO WORK HARD FOR YOU

Of course, there is always economics, and so there is always the possibility of giving people an *economic motive* for doing what you want them to do, even when they don't particularly care to do it otherwise. For instance, Little Willie has an older sister, Jill, and when he was a baby, she often wanted to play with her friends rather than play with Willie. But their mother promised Jill a quarter for every hour that Little Willie went through without crying. After that, somehow, Jill seemed to take a very real interest in keeping Little Willie happy. That 25¢ per hour *incentive* seemed to bring out quite a lot of motivation; and if the real motivation was to earn a quarter rather than to be nice to Little Willie, still, it seemed to produce pretty much the same results.

Controlling the Great Power of Incentives

Of course, one is not always able to secure the results one desires for 25¢ per hour, or even for a lot more. Some people, unfortunately, don't even do all they are paid to do; and in many situations it is not feasible even to offer to pay for the behavior one wants to bring about. In such cases, where the motivation does not already exist, there are two basic ways to approach a solution to the problem. One is to bring about the necessary motivation; the other is to find and offer an effective incentive that somehow fits into an existing but not necessarily related motivation.

Willie's father and mother were motivated to please him; they wanted to please him; they enjoyed pleasing him; they were happy when he was pleased. Under these circumstances it wasn't very difficult for Willie to get them to do what he wanted them to do.

(Anything within reason, for our darling boy!)

But now Willie has a boss, and this boss does not seem to be very markedly motivated to please Willie. In fact, the shoe appears to be upon the other foot: he expects Willie to try to please *him*!

Willie used to get what he wanted just by making clear what it was that he wanted, that getting it would please him, and that not getting it would make him unhappy. Such reasons or arguments as these were rather effective with his parents because they were already motivated to please him. But arguments similar to these seem to land with a dull thud when he tries them on his boss.

For instance, as a salesman, Willie wanted a territory assigned to him that would be convenient to his home, made up of better neighborhoods, and full of promising prospects. One territory, more nearly like that than the one he had, was already assigned to another salesman, Tod S. Willie made an appointment with his sales manager, and asked to be given Tod's territory.

Choosing the Right Incentive for the Situation

The sales manager was a rather shrewd character. He didn't just say no. He asked Willie: "Why? *Why* should I take Tod out of that territory, and put *you* in?" That question put it up to Willie to come up with a "good" reason—a reason that was not only "good" for Willie, but that would also seem "good" to the sales manager—one that would appeal to his existing motivations (concerning Willie or otherwise), or would provide him with an incentive that would be attractive to him on some other basis.

But Willie was too completely oriented to the approach that had been successful in the past—to appeals that were based upon his own wishes and desires. He explained to the sales manager how much more convenient Tod's territory would be *for him;* how much more pleasant it would be *for him* to work in that environment.

If Willie's father or mother had been the sales manager, that appeal might have been effective. But they weren't. If the sales manager had any motivations to please Willie, they were far outweighed by other considerations that were much more important *to him*. However, he realized that just his saying "No!" would be misunderstood by Willie as contrariness or antagonism; so he made the effort to straighten Willie out on the facts of life.

How Some People Reveal to You What Will Motivate Them

"Look here, Willie," he levelled, "I want you to understand that this company and this sales office are not being run for anybody's special benefit or pleasure. Not mine, not yours, not Tod's. No one's. Naturally, we're glad to do anything that helps one of our people, providing it makes good sense saleswise. That's what I'm interested in; that's *all* I'm interested in; and that's what *you* should be interested in. If I thought we'd get more sales by putting you in Tod's territory, I'd put you there in a minute. On the other hand, if I didn't think so, I wouldn't put you there—even if Tod wanted to swap territories with you—which he doesn't. Sales are what count around here, nothing else. So go and show me what you can do in the territory you have. I listen to the men who prove to me they can deliver the orders!"

Willie, of course, felt that the sales manager was unreasonable, unfeeling, and rude. But he was intelligent enough to realize that he was now in a new game, and if he wanted to win, he'd have to play by the new rules. So he went out and plugged away in his own territory. He studied the motivations of the sales manager and he looked for any arguments that would carry weight there. It took him a while, but he finally came up with a clincher. Then he asked for another meeting.

Making Others' Motives Work for Your Goal

"We are doing most of our business, now," Willie told the sales manager, "with manufacturers and contractors. But I have figured out that we have a big potential for our products and services among banks, insurance companies and other large office set-ups. We haven't been reaching this market. Now look at these figures. I've opened up 38 new accounts—and that's about all there is of this new kind of prospect in my territory. I've worked up an effective approach to these customers. I've been studying the whole subject, and now I'd like you to give me a territory where the potentials for this kind of business are bigger. I believe the biggest potential for this is in Tod's territory. How much of *this* kind of business is Tod getting there now?"

The sales manager was, of course, impressed. He checked up on Willie's sales, and found that Willie was right about his territory.

He saw an advantage that appealed *to him*—a chance for a substantial increase in sales—and so he gave Tod's territory to Willie. And Willie was more proud of that success than of anything he'd ever wheedled out of his family!

Three Objectives in Any Appeal to Basic Motivations

Willie had found a way to appeal to the sales manager's basic motivation—increased sales. To do this he had to accomplish several different but related objectives.

1. Find an idea that would give the sales manager what he wanted, so he would be motivated to act on it.
2. Find a way to tie that idea in to what Willie wanted, so that the sales manager would be motivated to give that to him.
3. Also, he had to build the sales manager's confidence in and respect for Willie. Without this, doubts would have killed the deal.

Willie had discovered a basic principle of how to motivate others to do what you want them to do, even when they are not motivated to do that just because you want them to. Willie found a constructive solution to his problem. He is pleased; the sales manager is pleased (only Tod is not so pleased, but even he may benefit in the long run).

3. HOW TO USE MOTIVATIONAL LEVERAGE TO GET WHAT YOU WANT FROM OTHERS

It was an ancient Greek, Archimedes, who siad, "Give me a place to stand on, and a lever that is long enough, and I can move the world." Archimedes understood the principle of *leverage*—as applied to the physical world. And moving people—motivating them to do as you want them to do—has certain characteristics in common with moving things.

How *Standing* Helps You to Move People

For instance, you have to have a place to stand. In the example previously given, Willie had a definite *standing:* he was a salesman, and he sold under the direction of the sales manager, who knew him to be capable and intelligent. With that background, he could use

the "lever" of the sales manager's own motivation—more sales—
by showing him how to get more sales by doing what Willie wanted
him to do. This even improved his *standing*.

If Willie had had a poor *standing* with the sales manager, his
idea would probably not have worked: the sales manager would not
entrust a potentially rich territory to an ineffective salesman. But
Willie was not satisfied just with demonstrating that he could
sell—he went on from there and demonstrated that he could sell
prospects who were not being sold (and who were numerous in the
territory he wanted).

In other words, Willie built up a big *advantage* for himself. He
used his ability and his idea and his opportunity to create a situation
where he had a lot of *leverage*—enough *leverage* to motivate the
sales manager to do what he wanted him to do.

How To Make Motivational *Leverage* Work for You

Through *leverage*, a small force can move a large weight.
Engineers call this "mechanical advantage." That is something like
the "Motivational Leverage" that can be used to motivate people.
The key to effectiveness in motivating people is a *"psychological
advantage."*

You may have all sorts of *advantages*, but the ones that count
are the ones that are important to the person you want to motivate.
For instance, Willie's sales manager plays a good game of golf.
Some of his other salesman play golf; they try, more or less, to
motivate the sales manager by playing golf with him. This doesn't
seem to give any of them a very great *advantage*.

How Willie Gained a Psychological *Advantage*

Willie happens to be rather good at tennis—but the sales manager couldn't care less about tennis. Thus, it was no *advantage* to
Willie, until it turned out that one of the best prospects in Willie's
new territory was a tennis "bug," and Willie started to get some
pretty good orders from him after they had played tennis together a
few times.

The sales manager was glad to O.K. Willie's expense account
for that; and suddenly Willie's skill at tennis became a real
advantage—with the sales manager. Before this could happen, the
sales manager had to see how it related to his own primary motiva-

tion and the primary basis for his interest in Willie—*more sales*!

The thing to do, of course, is to recognize as completely as possible the motivations that are important to the person you want to motivate, and then to see what you can do that will give you some *advantage* there.

How Al C. Won His Promotion

For instance, Al C. works in an office. He used to be a senior clerk in charge of a Unit, and now he is a supervisor. That promotion was no accident. Al carefully planned to motivate the Division Manager to promote him.

He studied the Division Manager carefully and he soon realized that this man was a zealot for accuracy. Mistakes really annoyed him. Clerical errors drove him wild (almost). He had a very low tolerance for failures in the correctness of paperwork. Al saw this powerful motivational tendency as his opportunity.

Al realized that if he could do anything to improve accuracy —to cut down on errors—he would be winning a lot of favorable recognition. So he thought about it a great deal. If he could offer a useful suggestion it would put him in a favorable light. That might help toward a promotion, but it might not be enough; others were already putting ideas into the suggestion system.

Al studied the office procedures, even those that were not directly involved in his own work. He saw that the Division Manager had set up a Special Unit to make corrections when mistakes came to light through customer complaints, calls or memos from other Divisions, etc. Al saw that the correction process bypassed the regular working Units: the corrections went from the Special Unit directly to the computer group, and so the Unit where the mistake had been made seldom even heard about their error. That gave Al his big idea.

He went to the head of the Special Unit and requested that he be informed of any errors made by his Unit. He made the appropriate arrangements with the head of the Special Unit, and then he began to receive copies of the necessary corrections. Each time, he traced the error to its source and went into it with the clerk who was responsible. He held regular conferences with his clerks to see how they could cut down on mistakes, and he kept score. Pretty soon he was able to see results.

Al then wrote up the whole story, and presented it to the Division Manager. He was able to show that he kept track of all errors made by his Unit that had to be corrected, and that in so doing he was reducing the incidence of such errors.

How Those Three Vital Objectives Worked Again

The Division Manager, naturally, was impressed. This appealed to him in his prime area of motivation. He asked questions, checked up personally, and soon announced Al's appointment as supervisor, with instructions to apply his corrective program over the whole Section.

So Al got what he wanted. And he earned it by showing the Division Manager that he—Al—could deliver more of what the Division Manager wanted. Al also had followed the same basic formula that got Willie his choice of territory.

1. Al found an idea that would give the Division Manager what he wanted, so he would be motivated to act on that idea.
2. Al found a way to tie that idea in to what *he* wanted, so that the Division Manager would be motivated to give that to him.
3. Al built his *standing* with the Division Manager by demonstrating initiative and showing what he could accomplish in an area of importance to the Division Manager, thus creating respect for and confidence in himself.

When all three of these factors were added together, Al got his promotion. He had created the *advantage* that gave him the *Motivational Leverage* he needed.

And it was all based upon Al's capitalization of his *advantage:* he was a senior clerk, in charge of a Unit. This gave him some *standing*–the opportunity to develop and try out his idea. The idea was his lever, and with this *advantage* he was able to motivate the Division Manager to promote him.

Most situations can provide some *advantage* toward motivating the boss to a promotion. In many cases, it isn't even necessary to find a new idea and make it work. Bosses are usually motivated to promote the person they think will do the best job. That kind of *standing* really counts! And *being* that person is usually the best way to motivate them to promote you. (But sometimes they need a little help, to see it!)

4. HOW TO BUILD ON YOUR ADVANTAGES
FOR GREATER MOTIVATIONAL LEVERAGE

In almost any situation, an individual who has any *standing* will have some *advantage,* and will therefore be in a position to apply motivational leverage. This advantage may not be a big one, and it may not even be easy to identify. But if you examine the situation with an open mind and think about it long enough, you should be able to think of something that gives you at least some chance of success in motivating favorably the person or persons you want to act in a certain way. It becomes, then, a question of using the *advantage* that is available to you.

Someone else may have a different *advantage*; often a better or bigger one. This may help them to get ahead of you, or even to work against your interests, if you are in competition. But remember that time is a great leveller and "shaker-upper." Conditions change, and sooner or later your *advantage* may be more important than theirs. So identify the *advantage* or *advantages* that are your best bet and find ways to apply them to your situation. Sooner or later they are quite likely to bring you something like the results you are seeking.

How Len T. Got Himself Appointed Manager

This point is illustrated by the story of Len T., now retired, as the principal owner of a large suburban automobile agency. Len got out of the Army in 1946, after a few tough years in New Guinea, the Philippines and Okinawa, and he got a job as an automobile salesman. The owner of the agency was elderly, and it was known that he was looking for a manager.

During World War II, of course, no automobiles were made for civilian use. There was a huge backlog of demand, and now that new cars were beginning to be available, everybody wanted one. The older salesmen, most of whom had not been in uniform, had long lists of friends, acquaintances and former customers who came to them actually begging for cars (deliveries were greatly delayed). Selling was not the problem—most customers would take anything they could get. But Len did have a problem—he didn't have a long list of friends, acquaintances and past customers.

He got his share of the customers that "just walked in," and he learned a lot about how to sell cars; but he realized that he was way behind the other salesmen in the number of cars sold. They had the prospects, and he didn't. He wasn't impressing the owner of the agency very favorably.

How to Use Your *Advantages* to Overcome *Dis-advantages*

Len had what seemed to be a *dis-advantage*. The more he thought about it, the more he realized that he had to overcome this handicap. So he went to work on it. He considered what *advantages* he had that he could use.

He was a veteran. He looked up all his old Army buddies that lived within a radius of an hour or so, and he joined the American Legion, the Veterans of Foreign Wars, etc.

He had attended schools in the area, and had been somewhat athletic, so he got involved in alumni gatherings, and looked up his old classmates and teammates.

He joined the church where he had gone to Sunday School, and set about meeting the other members of the congregation at socials, on committees, etc.

He found many other ways of enlarging his field of contacts.

He found that he had a certain flair for meeting people. He developed this until he had mastered the ways that please: he remembered faces and names; he remembered peoples' interests, hobbies, special concerns, relationships, etc. Gradually he developed a rather considerable acquaintance, and even gained some genuine friends. Many of these began to think of him when they thought of buying a car. He began to have quite a "following." The other salesmen began to notice this. And the owner of the agency took notice of this, as well.

How Changing Conditions Change *Advantages*—and *Dis-advantages*

Gradually the situation changed for automobile salesmen, as the initial demand was somehow met, and the supply began to meet current demand. Then customers found they could pick and choose and bargain.

Now the older salesmen were not doing so well. They had ridden along on the tide and they had not worked hard at keeping up their contacts and constantly building their following. Furthermore, many of their customers were resentful at having had to accept models or styles or colors they really didn't want—at top prices. And they hadn't gotten too much satisfaction when they had trouble or complaints. From now on it would take real work to be a success-ful automobile salesman.

The advantages that the older salesmen had had over Len now disappeared, and Len's hard work began to pay off. Now *he* had the *advantage*—an *advantage* that he had plugged for, starting from far behind. And he was now accustomed to put in time and effort, systematically, on building his contacts and his following, and on getting people to remember that he, Len, was the man to see when they needed a new car.

The owner of the agency observed all this shrewdly. He saw that Len was not an ordinary salesman, but a determined, purpose-ful, capable, forward-looking individual who had figured out what it took to sell cars, and was proving that he had learned the business and was making a success of it. After thinking about it a while, he called Len in and made him manager of the agency, with an over-riding commission on all cars sold.

How to Relate What You Do, to the Values of Others

Len had identified what *advantages* he had, and had used them to come from behind, and do better than those who had started with greater *advantages* than he. Len did not need an overwhelming *advantage*; he only needed enough to give him a chance. The change in market conditions brought out the difference in the ways Len and the others had exploited their *advantages*. The others had used theirs for an "easy ride"; Len used his to build *leverage*. Len came out on top because he took the trouble to figure what would motivate the owner, took hold of the right ideas to utilize what *advantages* he had, and earned himself the *standing* he needed.

Many a young man, employed by a large corporation and realizing that he is in competition with others for advancement, has been discouraged at the apparent *advantages* of his competitors—*advantages* that seem to make it much easier for them to win the favorable regard of management.

One such person, Bob S., faced the reality of his competition this way:

"I know J.S. has a much better education; and D.R. has had some valuable experience that I lack; and R.P. has terrific charm; and L.T. seems terribly bright. Perhaps they all have better chances than I have to impress the managers—(to motivate the managers to advance them).

"But," Bob went on in his private thoughts, "I think I have one *advantage* that may make all the difference for me, and I intend to use it as much as I can. My *advantage* is simply this: I am prepared and willing to try harder, to work more devotedly, to give it more effort, than the others. The time is bound to come when that will count—and count more than the *advantages* these other fellows have. When that time comes, Mr. Big will be motivated to pick *me*!"

You can motivate a waiter with a bigger tip. You can motivate a child with a toy or candy. You can motivate some people with gifts, or special attentions and courtesies, or even with bribes. But by and large you will have to motivate the people that count in your life by relating your own behavior to *their* values—to the values and interests that motivate them. That is the only way to real, effective *leverage*. And to do that, you will have to make the best use you can of the *advantages* that are yours to use.

5. HOW TO FIGURE YOUR "POTENTIALS" FOR GETTING WHERE AND WHAT YOU WANT

Earnest M. owned a prosperous business: he had a machining business that contracted or subcontracted to make metal parts of many kinds. The production end was divided into two shops, which had approximately equal numbers of employees, about the same equipment, and handled just about the same kinds and quantities of jobs. The foreman of Shop #1 was Archie N., and the foreman of Shop #2 was Aleck F. They were both very good men.

Archie and Aleck both wanted more pay and bigger bonuses. Both were a little tired of working late hours—and sometimes weekends—to catch up on the paperwork that was a necessary part of their jobs, especially when Earnest took on rush orders, as he frequently did. Both of them got what they wanted, but they went after it differently, and so, in the end, one got a lot more than the other.

How Archie N. Got His Bonus

Archie figured that his *advantage* was that he was indispensable. He was doing a good job, he was making a lot of money for Earnest, and Archie knew that Earnest was motivated to keep it going that way. So he went to Earnest, made his demands for more pay and a bigger bonus, complained about the long hours, and threatened to quit if he didn't get what he wanted.

Earnest gave in—he really was motivated to keep things going the way they were, so he agreed to give Archie what he wanted. Success for Archie: he identified an *advantage*, spotted the boss's prime motivation, and hooked what he wanted on to what the boss wanted. With that *leverage* Archie got what he was after, because the boss was more motivated to keep Archie on than to let him go.

How Aleck F. Did Even Better

But Aleck went at it rather differently. He studied the situation and saw everything that Archie saw—even considered going the same route (and he would have been equally successful). But Aleck thought he ought to go beyond that, and be constructive about it by giving Earnest something extra, in exchange for what he wanted. He wanted to appeal to more of Earnest's motivations than just Earnest's fear of losing him.

Aleck realized that Earnest was spending a lot of time on his own paperwork, and that much of Earnest's paperwork took up where Aleck's left off. When Aleck's paperwork was late, Earnest got started late. When Aleck's paperwork was rough, sketchy, hard to follow or even hard to read, Earnest was handicapped. Earnest understood that Aleck's work as foreman—getting out the work —came first; and so he seldom complained when Aleck's paperwork was late or hastily prepared. But Aleck knew that this cost Earnest extra time, effort and annoyance, and that he often stayed late in his office, or took work home.

How You Can Make Your *Standing* with Others Pay Off for You Through Greater Motivational Leverage

Aleck also realized that getting out special and rush orders left little time for his other responsibilities—principally cutting costs, and good maintenance of equipment. Again, Earnest understood the problem; but it was also understood that cost control and maintenance generally left something to be desired, and production took priority.

Aleck knew, however, that Earnest would be motivated toward improvement in these areas. So he prepared himself to use these motivations, plus his *standing* and *advantages* as foreman, to exert *leverage* to get what he wanted for himself. He asked Earnest to name a time when they wouldn't be interrupted, and he went in and made his pitch.

"Earnest," he began, "I've been thinking about things, especially about cutting costs and improving maintenance, and I have an idea that ought to appeal to you. You know I put in long hours on production—just on getting the work out, and we haven't been doing badly. You get the jobs and we take them on. And even when we run into overtime, we must be making a tidy profit.

"But that profit could be bigger. I figure we could cut costs at least 10% if I could spend another hour or two a day on that.

"And if I could get after maintenance a little more, we could up production quite a bit. For instance, we have machines down for repair; if I could put in a good program of preventive maintenance, we would have more effective capacity. Now, are you interested?"

"Hell, yes!" Earnest replied. "Good thinking so far—keep going!"

"Well, I can set up and run a good cost reduction program; and I can put in and run the preventive maintenance program; but it will take more time—and I'm putting in 50-to 60-hour weeks right now.

"So—Earnest—I want some help. I want to put Frank in charge of maintenance—that'll take him off his regular job about five hours a week; and I want Leo and Tom to come in four hours on Saturdays. I figure we can save at least three times as much as that will cost. O.K.?"

"O.K.! Good—go to it! And where does that save your time?" Earnest asked.

"I'm coming to that. There's a lot of paperwork to cutting costs. I think we need help there. I'd like you to hire a good, smart, young clerk, with some accounting experience. He can help me with all my regular paperwork, and the cost control, too. You'll get my work a lot sooner, and in a lot better shape—and I know that won't make your wife mad!

"Another thing—I probably won't need that clerk full time. He can put in some time helping you or Archie. I figure, in my shop we ought to be able to cut costs at least four times the clerk's pay. What do you say?"

"Well, Aleck, let's try it. It sounds good to me; and if we can really save all that much by better maintenance and cost control, we should. You go ahead with Frank and Leo and Tom, and I'll start trying to hire a useful clerk. And thanks, Aleck. Anything else?"

"Well, yes, there is, Earnest. Seems like these ideas are going to put quite a few more dollars into the profits; and not too many of them come out of there, to me. Couldn't we do something about that?"

"Well, Aleck, I guess you've got it coming to you. So—you'll find your check has grown a little bigger, beginning this week. And come the end of the year, you'll get, say, a third of what we save through the new maintenance and cost control programs. Does that help?"

How to Figure the "Potentials" for Best Results

Aleck actually got more for himself by his approach to his boss than Archie did, and, in addition, he built himself some excellent new *standing*—which Archie didn't. Archie had used his *standing* (as a good foreman) in such a way as to impair it. By threatening to quit he had hurt his relationship with Earnest, who now felt that Archie was motivated entirely by getting more money. On the other hand, Aleck had made Earnest feel that he was really motivated to do a good job and to be helpful; Earnest even made a mental note that Aleck might make a good general manager for the business when Earnest felt more like retiring, in a few years.

So Aleck really made the most of his *advantages*, and he gained accordingly. Archie, by contrast, gave up quite a bit to gain what he wanted. He hurt his *standing* and gave up a lot of his principal *advantage* in order to motivate his boss—*this* time. *Next* time Archie threatens to quit, Earnest will probably let him do it.

When you want to motivate others, use your *standing* and your *advantages;* but use them thoughtfully. Remember you may want to use them again.

Use them creatively; don't use them *up!* And in that way you can build more *standing,* as you go.

2

APPLYING MOTIVATIONAL
LEVERAGE TO CHANNEL
THE BEHAVIOR OF OTHERS

If you are going to apply Motivational Leverage effectively, you have to know something about the person or persons to whom you will be applying it. In fact, you may have to know and understand quite a good deal about them, in order to be sure that the Motivational Leverage you want to apply will really be applicable. This chapter can help you to develop and apply your Motivational Leverage on a sound basis.

1. HOW TO PREVENT UNEXPECTED BEHAVIOR

When we are concerned about motivating another person, it is usually because something they are doing—or not doing—is unsatisfactory to us, and we want them to behave differently. And, of course, we want to motivate them not only to stop doing (or not doing) whatever is unsatisfactory to us, but also to start behaving in a way that *will* satisfy us.

In order to motivate people effectively, naturally, you first have to understand *WHY* they are behaving as they are; and then you need to understand what could get them to change in the way you want them to; and then you have to figure out how to get them to make that change. Three steps, in all.

All this may require quite a lot of study, before you develop the necessary insights. On the other hand, sometimes it is surprisingly easy. Many people, when they seek to motivate others, act rather blindly out of impatience, frustration, eagerness, ignorance, etc. Sometimes they are lucky, sometimes not. But the best way is to be sure you really have an adequate understanding of the situation— that you *really* know what is *really* going on.

Dealing with the Unexpected

Mabel D. was office manager of a real estate agency, in charge of six employees. The owner, Sam B., was elderly, and beginning to take it easy. Mabel was taking over more and more responsibilities, and soon she realized that Sam was beginning to depend more and more on her to handle many matters he used to handle himself. She began to feel that she was not only more valuable, but even indispensable; and so she decided to demand a very substantial raise.

The way she read the situation, Sam would have to give it to her. He would be irresistibly motivated to do so, because he would have to recognize that he had no practical alternative: he couldn't manage without her.

So Mabel picked her time—right after he had given her extensive instructions covering the next week, when he would be away—and she stated her case and made her demand. Old Sam just looked at her; he remained silent for what seemed a long time. Then he smiled, and said he'd think about it while he was away.

When Sam came back he told her he was about to retire, was moving to Florida, and was selling the agency to a competitor. He promised Mabel that he would give her a strong recommendation to the take-over firm.

Suddenly Mabel realized that she must have left a few things out of her calculations. She hadn't waited to make sure she knew the situation fully—what was *really* going on.

Understanding Something That Will Help
You to Apply Motivational Leverage More Effectively

It turned out that Sam had been thinking vaguely about retirement ("maybe in a few years"), but Mabel's sudden demand had triggered a decision to do it now. When it was too late, she realized that she should have motivated Sam by showing him how she could take over more and more of the management of the agency, so that he would have felt like keeping on, while taking it easier. As it was, she had forced his decision to retire by facing him with a demand which did not really fit into his motivations very well.

She *thought* he would be motivated by the realization that he could not operate without her. That motivation existed, potentially—*if* he wanted to keep on operating. But it was dependent upon the motivation to operate at all. Without *that* basic motivation, the dependent motivation that she counted on could not have any effect. And she had badly miscalculated the motivation that turned out to be basic.

How "Doing Your Homework" Can Really Pay Off

Obviously, Mabel had not done her homework. She should have thought along these lines: "Sam is getting old, and is beginning to take it easy. I'm picking up the load, more and more. Where is this leading? How long will Sam want to keep going? How much more will he want me to take over? Will he feel like retiring? How soon? If and when he does, what arrangements will he make? Will he close up the agency, sell it off, or what?"

If Mabel had thought in that way, she might have felt that the best way for her to motivate Sam was to be more and more helpful; to make herself more and more indispensable. In the end, she might be practically running the agency—and then she might be able to make a deal with Sam to take it over. As it was, she was practically back where she had started, years before.

Mabel should have asked herself more about Sam's motivations. And she should have looked for the answers not in her own wishful thinking but in objectively observing Sam's behavior, and analyzing the reasons behind it clearly, and without "kidding" herself.

When Sam turned over new responsibilities to her, she had

been reacting subjectively: "How much more important I am, here!" instead of figuring out carefully *why* Sam was passing on to her each particular responsibility.

If Mabel had done this, she would have been able to realize that he was passing on the more time-consuming, the more detailed and wearying duties. He was conserving his own energies for the activities that brought *in* the money—getting listings, attracting buyers, showing properties, handling sales and closings. She was getting all the supporting paperwork—essential, but not the primary activities of the business.

Mabel should have made a greater effort to understand Sam's actual motivations—what was *really* going on—even if Sam hadn't crystallized his own planning yet. After that happened, it would probably be too late to motivate him otherwise.

Being Careful With Other People's Motivations

To take another example: Mrs. Barlow T. is elderly and quite wealthy, and she depends a great deal upon younger relatives—even some distant cousins—plus paid companions, nurses, servants, etc. She is motivated to have people do all sorts of things for her and look after her in various ways. Those around her are motivated by all sorts of values, running all the way from respect, loyalty, affection or sense of duty, to pay and to the expectation or hope of inheritance.

Mrs. T. is sensitive, and suspicious. She likes to feel that everyone is motivated "unselfishly." When she gets the idea that anyone is interested in her only for "selfish" reasons, she turns against them; she even changes her will. So if anyone is motivated to attend on Mrs. T. by the expectation of a bequest, that motivation is enough to kill the bequest (if Mrs. T. suspects it).

This, of course, is a complex situation, where people are motivated to conceal their motivations. But such situations are extremely common.

There is the boss who is motivated to get all he can out of a number of competing subordinates. Each of these is motivated to surpass the others in his eyes. But they conceal their competitive motivations from one another, and act in a friendly, comradely manner among themselves. The boss, even after he has decided which one he will promote, conceals this decision as long as possible in order to keep them all trying hard.

Then there is the customer who wants a lower price, but who pretends he is not strongly motivated to buy; and the seller who is strongly motivated to sell to his only prospect, but tries to give the impression that he is besieged with good offers.

Life is full of situations where motives are hidden, disguised, complex, confused, obscure, and even surprising. Anyone interested in motivating others should not too readily assume that he fully understands their motivation. It is too easy to be wrong.

2. HOW TO MAKE OTHERS REVEAL THE HIDDEN REASONS FOR ACTING AS THEY DO

In order to understand what is really going on so that you can plan to motivate someone successfully, you need to know *and to understand WHY* they act as they do. You can always think of some possible reason why; and it is easy to fall into the trap of *believing* you understand the motivation of another, when in fact you are deceiving yourself, if not entirely, then at least enough to put your judgment off about what you should do.

One of the best ways of understanding the motivation of others is to look for the *causes* of their behavior. Ask yourself *WHY* they behave as they do: *WHY* they do something, or *WHY* they fail to do something, or *WHY* they do it in a certain way. Then, when you have thought of an answer, weigh it; check it against the known facts, and if it does check, ask yourself if perhaps there is some other factor that has not yet come to your notice, which might change the answer. Give *this* enough thought. Then, if you are still satisfied with the answer, ask yourself *WHY*, again. And, in all of this, try to be objective: try to keep *yourself* out of your answers; try to put yourself in the other fellow's place. If you do all this carefully and well, you should come up with a realistic appreciation of the motivations of the person you want to motivate.

A Better Idea for Mabel D.

For example, in the case given in the preceding section, Mabel D. recognized that her boss, Sam B., was delegating more and more of his work *to her*. She was more aware of the specific fact that he was delegating *to her* than of the basic, general fact that *he was delegating*. So she overlooked the basic fact that he *wanted to delegate.* She saw a few trees, instead of the woods.

When she asked herself *WHY* he was doing as he did, the answer she gave herself emphasized more the idea that he wanted to delegate *to her* than that he *wanted to delegate.* And so, when she asked herself *WHY* he wanted to delegate *to her*, she came up with the answer that he trusted her, had confidence in her, depended on her, etc. This, of course, led her to think she had an *advantage* she could use to motivate him to give her a big raise.

How to See Other People's Reasons More Clearly

But if she had left herself out of the picture, she could have come up with better answers. In the first place, when she asked herself *WHY* he was doing as he did, the basic answer should have been simply that *he wanted to delegate.* If she then asked *WHY* he wanted to delegate, and put herself in his place, she would quite naturally have thought, in terms of *his* position, that he was getting older, and wanted to take it easy. That should have led her to realize the possibility that he might be thinking of retiring, selling out, and so forth.

After she had recognized Sam's basic motivation, that he wanted to delegate, Mabel could then have asked herself *WHY* he delegated *certain particular responsibilities.* Then she would have realized that he was delegating *only the responsibilities he knew she could handle.* Once she realized that clearly, she could begin to think about *other responsibilities*—the really important ones. Was he motivated also to delegate those? How? To whom?

If Mabel had followed this line of analysis, she would have understood that Sam was motivated to look for the best way to turn over all or most of his responsibilities; and then she could have worked on using her very real *advantage* to fit this basic motivation of Sam's. Instead, she faced him with an expensive demand just when he was thinking about retiring and turning over the agency to someone else.

Mabel made the big, basic mistake of not seeking real causes. She saw her *advantage*, and she tried to use it, without really understanding the motivations of the person she wanted to motivate. This is a very common mistake. Don't make it. Ask yourself *WHY*, and "leave yourself out," to find objective, realistic answers until you really understand the motivations you intend to work on.

How to Figure Out Reasons Behind Strange Reactions

George G. was a young engineer who was just starting on a new job with the Custer Manufacturing Company. He was somewhat confused and bewildered, as he had not been with a manufacturing company before; he had been in construction. He needed and wanted helpful, friendly, knowledgeable guidance, counseling and advice.

The person in the best position to offer this kind of help was an older engineer, Arthur D., whose desk was near his in the engineering office. But Arthur was rather cool and stand-offish and did not encourage George's first friendly advances. George began to think about how to motivate Arthur to unbend, and to become friendly and helpful. He began to observe Arthur carefully.

He noticed that Arthur was not really friendly with anyone in the engineering office except one draftsman, and he asked himself why. He made it a point to get into a few conversations with the draftsman, and learned that he was an amateur astronomer, and very enthusiastic about his hobby. The next time George saw Arthur and the draftsman having coffee together in the plant cafeteria, he found an excuse to go over with a question for the draftsman, and he soon realized that the two were talking astronomy. They were discussing their hobby projects: they were both building reflecting telescopes at home.

George began to ask himself questions. *WHY* was Arthur so aloof? Apparently, that was his nature; he was not a gregarious, out-going person. But then, *WHY* was he friendly with the draftsman? Apparently because they had an interesting hobby in common. *WHY* did that make Arthur friendly? Probably because it gave him something to talk about—he had no small talk, and he was pretty much the silent type. Then, finally, *WHY* was Arthur cool to George? Mainly because that was his nature; partly because other young engineers had bothered him and been uninteresting to him; partly because he had nothing to say.

How You Can Operate More Surely

Armed with these objective answers about the causes of Arthur's behavior, George began to look for an *advantage* that he might use to motivate Arthur to ''loosen up'' with him. He had taken a course in optics at engineering school. He dug out his old textbooks and refreshed himself on the optics and characteristics of reflecting telescopes, and on lens grinding and on parabolic mirrors.

When he felt that he had sufficiently fortified himself, he invited the draftsman to lunch with him, and soon led the conversation around to the man's hobby. George led him to speak enthusiastically of his progress in the construction of the telescope; and then less enthusiastically about some of the problems and difficulties he was encountering with it.

Then George began to talk knowledgeably about the matter. He revealed that he had studied optics, and spoke helpfully about lens grinding. The draftsman was fascinated and delighted, and the luncheon was a protracted one.

Next day Arthur, almost with embarrassment, came over to George. "I understand you know quite a lot about optics," he said.

George returned a modest answer, and then Arthur asked: "I wonder if you could explain something to me"—and proceeded to outline a question about certain parameters of parabolic reflectivity.

George gave him a careful, general reply, and promised to bring him a more complete answer the next day, after checking with his old textbooks.

Arthur turned out to be a very decent, solid, helpful person; quiet and "hard to know," but well worth knowing. George got from him all the help and advice he wanted.

George's success with Arthur was based on his search for causes. He didn't take Arthur's coolness personally; he looked for what was behind it all. When he learned of something that was really motivating Arthur, he began to look for an *advantage*, and he found it. He couldn't have been successful in motivating Arthur as he wished, if he had not gone back to the *causes* of Arthur's behavior.

3. GAINING DEEP UNDERSTANDING OF PEOPLE'S MOTIVATIONS

People generally try to do what they want to do, and this provides an element of consistency in actions that are actually unrelated. For instance, Oscar G. is a young clerk who is ambitious to become office manager. This motivation enters into many of the things he does, whether they seem connected with his ambition or not; and if this motivation is understood, the reasons why Oscar behaves as he does, in many situations, become easier to understand.

As an example, on a Saturday night Oscar and his girl-friend, Irene, went to a party at the home of one of her friends. There were a lot of young people there, of course, and many of them held lower level positions in various offices. When they talked about their jobs and their experiences at work, many of them boasted about the way they had "put one over" on the supervisor or the office manager. They told stories about how stupid or arbitrary, how unreasonable and unfair their bosses were; and—often—how they had "out-smarted" their bosses, and "gotten away with it."

There was much laughing and joining in with this kind of talk, but Oscar did not laugh, and Oscar did not join in. Even when invited by others to tell about episodes of a similar nature in his own experience, Oscar refrained. In fact, he left the circle where these stories were being exchanged, and showed a strong preference for mingling with other guests, who had not been actively engaged in this interchange of "anti-boss" sentiments.

Irene, of course, noticed this, and on the way home in Oscar's car she commented on it, reproaching him. Oscar was quite willing to explain his behavior.

Getting Where You Want to, by Thinking on the Level You Want to Reach

"Some people go to work in offices as clerks," he pointed out, "and they stay clerks. That's because they think like clerks, and they think of themselves as clerks. That way, they'll probably never be promoted, because they haven't got what it takes to be a boss. They think it's smart to 'goof off,' or get away with something, or 'put one over.' But the mean little ego-satisfaction they may get from that is all the good it will do them.

"If you want to be a boss, Irene, you have to think like a boss, even when you're not. You have to have a feeling about responsibilities for results. You have to be interested in getting things done. And when you feel *that* way, Irene, then the kind of talk those kids were putting out tonight is just silly. It's childish. Of course, some of the juniors in my office do the same thing; but not me! I'm thinking about getting promoted. I try not to be like those silly kids."

Studying People's Behavior to Understand Their Hidden Purposes

Oscar wants to be a boss, so he *identifies* with management: he tends to take the point of view of his superiors; to accept *their* values and interests and objectives; to think about things as he would if he were now—as he intends to be later—a boss himself. So Oscar's motivation in the office carries over, and influences his behavior at a party.

You might wonder about Oscar's behavior at the party, as his girl-friend did, if you did not know about his ambitions, and so did not see the connection. But if you did know about his ambitions, the connection would not be hard to see.

However, most of the time people do not explain their motivations to us. We have to figure them out for ourselves: we have to *infer* the motivations from what they do and say—from their behavior. The young men and women in the noisy group who noticed Oscar's non-participation must have had all kinds of reactions. Some of them merely assumed that he was aloof, or too solemn by nature; others may have believed that something was troubling him—that he had something else on his mind. A few may have recognized that he didn't find the conversation interesting, that somehow he didn't share the general attitude of the others toward their work and its involvements.

They might have asked themselves *WHY*? And some of them might have been able to figure out the reason—that Oscar's motivation to become a boss put him out of sympathy with anti-boss attitudes.

"Oscar is ambitious," they might have observed. "He plans to get ahead—fast! He has no time for kidding around. He doesn't think that way. He's serious. All he thinks about is how to move up!" Such an analysis would explain a lot of Oscar's behavior, off the job as well as on. It would even explain why he stopped seeing Irene and began to be serious about Irma, who was also goal-oriented and serious.

So Oscar's underlying motivation explains many different kinds of his behavior—from performance on the job to selection of girl-friends. His motivation provides a basis of consistency for all of the things he does. Once you understand Oscar's motivation, you understand *him* better; and you understand why he does things; and you get to see ways in which you can *use* his motivation to get him to do what you want him to do.

How Understanding People's Motivations Helps You to Influence Their Behavior

If you are Oscar's boss, you can encourage Oscar to almost any length of hard work and special effort by suggesting that such activities will help on the path to advancement. If you are Oscar's girl-friend, you can motivate him to increasing interest in you by sympathizing with and approving his advancement goals; by encouraging him in them; and by showing that you share his attitudes and values. Also, by showing him that you are not frivolous and shortsighted, but earnest, and by showing him that you take a long-term view of life.

However desirable it may be to go from understanding a person's motivation to understanding why a person acts as he does, we usually have to go in the other direction. We can observe a person's behavior, try to figure out why they act as they do, and so attempt to arrive at an understanding of their motivation.

Sometimes this requires a lot of study. It is easy to ascribe a motivation for an act; it is not always easy to ascribe one that fits the reality. For example, in the previous section, Mabel D. found this out when she made her mistake about Sam B. It is a common kind of error. It must be guarded against.

How to Avoid Mistakes by Recognizing the Ideas Behind People's Actions

The best way to guard against such mistakes is to check the supposed motivation against a number of different kinds of behavior of the same person. For instance, at the party, after Oscar left the "anti-boss" group, he joined another, smaller group that was talking about computers. The members of this group were interested in the changes occurring in offices when operations were computerized. Some of those in the group were programmers; one worked at the delineation of methods and procedures; the others worked in offices where the introduction of computers had brought about significant changes.

Oscar had entered into the conversation quite actively. He had shown intense interest, had listened attentively, and had contributed several times in such a way as to arouse the interest of the group.

It was clear, even to Irene, that whatever had been the motivation behind Oscar's behavior with the first group, it was not working the same way with the second group.

Of course, Oscar might have been acting on the basis of short-term motivations—like or dislike of individuals in the groups, desire to participate, to "belong," to leave early, etc. But whatever consistent motivations might be involved, clearly they were negative to the first group and positive to the second.

Anyone observing Oscar's behavior in a greater number of groups would have a good chance to figure out what kind of talk caused him to have negative reactions, and what aroused positive reactions. And from this, they ought to be able to make a pretty good guess at the underlying motivations.

4. HOW TO SEE CLEARLY WHAT MAKES A PERSON "TICK"

People are moved by an infinite variety of motives, but most of these can be grouped under a few major headings. All of us, probably, are more or less subject to most of these kinds of motivation. But each of us is more vulnerable to some kinds of motivation than to others, and our vulnerability to any one kind may vary from extreme to negligible. In fact, we may have such scorn for some kinds of motivation that we feel like doing exactly the opposite of what they call for.

Analyzing What Fear Does to People

Take, as an example, "fear." Fear can be a very powerful motivation. The business man who is threatened with physical violence by racketeers may be motivated to do whatever they ask of him. On the other hand, some men are very brave—or very stubborn. They would despise themselves if they gave in to threats. In the even more extreme case of armed hold-ups, some people, motivated by fear (they may call it prudence) eagerly give up everything they have in the hope of avoiding physical injury. Yet others will be motivated to resist, even to attack the armed criminals; and their motivation may be a kind of fear of fear—a strong aversion to being afraid. But a man who defies a threat of physical violence to himself may yield, in terror, to a threat of injury to his family.

Fear of physical injury is not a very usual motivation in ordinary, law-abiding circumstances, of course. And yet fear enters into many motivations. Many people are insecure. They are afraid of losing their jobs, of being reprimanded, of being embarrassed, of losing status, even of being wrong, or looking foolish. Some people are very strongly motivated by such considerations, often in a negative way. Fears of such kinds often prevent people from doing what they might like to do—what might be best for them or for the organization. Fear keeps people silent when they ought to be heard; fear keeps people inactive when they ought to act. Fear keeps people from "sticking their necks out," from taking chances. Fear keeps people from trusting others.

Such conditions are quite common, and when people are motivated by such fears, it is easy to use those fears to motivate them in the direction their fears are driving them. As an example, suppose an employee wants to persuade a supervisor to try out a new operating procedure that involves other employees; and suppose also that another employee is opposed to the idea. That second employee can go to the supervisor and point out the consequences of failure: lost time and effort, making a conspicuous mistake, being criticized by higher levels of management, etc. If the supervisor is easily motivated by fear, he will decide not to run the risks of the experiment. If he has the courage of his convictions, he will go ahead—cautiously and step by step, perhaps, but still, he will go ahead. Another motivation will outweigh fear.

Harnessing the Power of the Ego to Move People

Many of the most important sources of motivation, of course, are those involving the individual's ego: his desire for status and for admiration; his drive to be conspicuously successful in the eyes of others. This is an extremely common kind of motivation, though in its specific forms it may vary from a housewife's entering her own prize recipe in a cooking contest, to a politician's aiming at the White House. People tend to be motivated favorably toward whatever will "build them up," and quite unfavorably toward anything that will "tear them down."

Such motivations as these are so basic that they are among those most commonly used to influence people; but, also, they are so much in effect, normally, on all of us that it is not always easy to bring a new aspect to bear, in order to effectuate a particular purpose.

For instance, a manager of a large division of a major company must nominate his successor, since he is himself moving up to a vice-presidency in corporate headquarters. He must choose between Arnold G. and Rollo S. Both of them, of course, are trying to influence him, and he is quite concerned about making a wise choice. If the one he names should turn out to be less than satisfactory, it will reflect unfavorably on him, so he is strongly motivated to select the one who will perform best. But which one is that? It is not easy to decide.

Finally Rollo finds occasion to remind the manager that it was he, the manager, who hired Rollo in the first place, twelve years ago; and that Rollo held his first position with the company, had his first training for greater responsibilities and recieved his first promotion under this same manager. The manager thus has a greater personal stake in Rollo than in Arnold. That makes a difference. Rollo has found a way to motivate the manager, using his special *advantage* on the manager's ego-motivation. "Rollo is really *my* boy," the manager is thinking.

How to Use Results-Oriented Motivation to Get the Results You Want

Another important kind of motivation is based upon the desire to achieve certain results; to attain certain objectives; to work toward certain goals. A person who is really interested in working toward making something happen will tend to be motivated favorably toward anything that can help. He will evaluate alternatives in terms of their effects on the progress of the project he favors. Typically, a politician who is running for office will be inclined to favor and to make promises to those who support him; he may even think in terms of penalizing those who do not.

Goal orientations, however, are not always clear-cut. For instance, the purpose of a business organization is to make a profit. But some executives seem to do more thinking about how to advance their own interests than how to make the business more profitable; and in some organizations there really can be a substantial divergence. Anyone working under such an extremely self-seeking superior should be aware that he will not necessarily regard service to the company as service *to him*.

How to Go Beyond Using Money as a Motivator

Of course we must recognize that money is a prime source of motivation. Since it is the common denominator of everything that can be bought, it represents the most comprehensive potential for things people want, and so has an extremely broad appeal. Nevertheless, it has its severe limitations.

To begin with, in many situations it is simply not feasible to use money as a motivating factor, because that would involve bribery or corruption. Promotions and selection for particular assignments in organizations, for instance, are not supposed to be subject to such influences. And yet such situations are commonly the focus of serious—and generally ethical and legitimate—efforts to motivate a decision in a particular direction.

Price cutting, bargain sales and discounts are common methods for motivating people to buy. Salaries, wages, commissions, bonuses, fees and other kinds of payments are common methods of getting people to do what you want them to do. People take all sorts of risks and chances to "make money." They undergo all sorts of discomforts and difficulties, even hardships and risk, for pay or other reward—or even for the hope of it. People spend their lives at work that can afford them little inherent satisfaction—even for what seems to be very little money. Surely we cannot overlook money as the obvious, typical motivation.

But it is still true that other motivations are basic, vital and of the greatest importance, and, in many situations, more effective than money. People who are *too* influenced by money are said to be venal, "money-mad," "hungry." They are too often cheats, misers, or coldly calculating "bloodsuckers." They alienate others, who are repelled by them. Their crassness, their sheerly materialistic outlook robs them of all other satisfactions; they find nothing in life but the stark enjoyment of accumulation, by any means.

There are so many values in life on which no price in dollars can be placed. There are so many men and women who cannot be "bought"; who make their choices and decisions on the basis of principle, of intelligent self-interest, and of the good of others. They are not without interest in money—far from it. But they value much besides; and anyone who wishes to motivate them must understand the other motivational forces that affect their behavior and influence their actions.

5. HOW TO FIT YOUR MOTIVATIONAL LEVERAGE TO THE INDIVIDUAL

Mr. J. K. L., Junior, was president and chief executive officer of Apex Fabrications, Inc., a diversified manufacturing company making an excellent profit on a growing annual turnover that was over $40,000,000 the previous year. J.K. was the son of the founder of the business; and his father, now in his seventies, was still Chairman of the Board of Directors, and still kept track of things.

After a lot of recent growth, J.K. had some problems with his executives. At the time in question, he was concerned about Ralph D., who had recently been assigned to manage the Western Division.

How Ralph D. Reacted

Ralph formerly had the position of vice-president for manufacturing, which was really a staff coordinating job, since the divisions produced different product lines, and the manager of each manufacturing division was responsible for its profitability. Six months previously, Ralph had been transferred from his post at company headquarters in New York City to the job of General Manager of the Western Division, with offices and principal plant in a small town in Nebraska.

The Western Division was the largest but not the most profitable division. It accounted for almost half the company's gross income, but less than a quarter of the net profit. The previous General Manager of the division had been unable to improve matters. He had been switched with Ralph, and was now in the New York headquarters with Ralph's old job.

After six months, J.K. could see few signs of improvement. He was quite disappointed: he had expected a great deal from Ralph. And he was wondering what to do about it, one day, when his father, in the office on one of his frequent visits, asked about that very matter.

J.K. was glad of a chance to discuss it with his father, whose insights often proved valuable. He showed the reports, messages, correspondence and memos. He went over the summary figures for the six-month period, and for previous periods, and particularly over Ralph's sales and production forecasts and proposed budget for the upcoming fiscal year.

"I can't see here that Ralph expects much improvement," J.K. commented, finally. "And what bothers me even more—I don't see that he is really trying very hard. Back here in the head office Ralph was always 'rarin' to go'—an eager beaver—a regular tiger, and all that. Now, if you read his reports and talk to him on the telephone, it seems like all the steam has gone out of him. You know that division needs a real shaking up. I thought Ralph could do it. But he'd have to go after it a lot differently than he is doing now. I'm really disappointed."

His father was silent for a minute. Then he commented briefly.

"Ralph could do it—if he *really* wanted to."

J.K. was surprised, almost shocked. "What do you mean '*if* he *really* wanted to'? Ralph was always ambitious—anxious to show what he could do. I promised him a nice bonus and a big raise if he could get that division going, and I increased his stock option. What more could he expect?"

How Motivations Work Differently with Different People

"Well," his father replied, "you yourself seem to think he's lost his motivation. That means something, doesn't it? Whatever you offered or promised him, it hasn't done the job of getting him to do what you wanted him to."

J.K. Junior had to admit his father was right about that. And then the older man really surprised him. "I think I'll go out there and visit with Ralph a bit," he said.

Ralph D. was rather fond of J.K. Senior, and genuinely glad to see him. After a day in the office and plant, the older man dined with Ralph and Ralph's wife in their home, and after dinner they excused themselves and retired to Ralph's study with their brandy and cigars. After a while, Ralph found himself talking quite plainly and frankly to his very patient and understanding companion.

"Your son thinks he can just push buttons to control people," Ralph declared. "He decided he wanted me to come out here and manage this division, when Jeff couldn't show an improvement in it. So he calls me in and tells me I'm due out here October first. That was it, really. Of course, he sweetened it with sweet-talk and a raise and a bigger stock option, and promises of a bonus; but that was the least he could do. Then he puts Jeff in my old job, in the head office, and here I am, out in the boondocks. My wife hates it here, and so do I. We're big city people.

"OK, so it's a big opportunity for me to show what I can do. So, suppose I show it? What happens? Do I get to stay out here, and keep up the good work? Great! Or do I go back to my old job? After Jeff has had it, who fizzled out here? Any way you figure it, I lose. Sure, I come into some extra dollars, but that isn't everything. I'm only 42. I have to think about the future. I'm out of touch, here. It's just *not what I want*!"

Making the Motivation Fit the Individual

"What *do* you want, Ralph?" the older man asked, quietly.

"I could do a better job of moving the Western Division ahead, from New York, than from here. We can put in a plant superintendent who can cut costs and improve methods and handle all the really local problems. What this division needs is new products, better designs, and a lot hotter marketing—and all that can be done a great deal better from New York than from here. I'm handicapped, here, away from the real marketplace; away from the experts and specialists I need to get a new product line going; away from the pulse of things.

"Make me Executive Vice-President. Put me in the New York office, with complete authority over this division. If I don't deliver, fire me!"

The Chairman of the Board could see that the President had completely muffed the ball, when it came to motivating the man he had counted on to rehabilitate the company's largest division. J.K. Junior had believed that he was providing adequate motivation in the form of opportunity supported by financial incentives. But to Ralph, it was not a *real* opportunity; the financial incentives were not very significant, and he felt resentment at being manipulated and physically shifted to an uncongenial environment. In effect, he had been motivated to mark time, even to sulk. Certainly he had not been made to feel like throwing all the resources of his knowledge, skill, intelligence, experience and energy into the job that J.K. Junior expected him to do.

On the other had, it was clear that Ralph wanted real authority, properly symbolized by status, and he wanted to be near the seats of power. He wanted to concern himself with the decisive, the creative, the constructive; not with routine administration. He wanted to make policy, not merely to execute it. And he was willing to stake his career on the outcome.

One Good Way of Motivating People

Clearly, J.K. had misread the situation. He had not used the motivations that would have been right for Ralph. He could have avoided his error and learned the best way to handle the situation with Ralph *if* he had called Ralph in for an open-end discussion, instead of telling him what he had decided; *if* he had let Ralph participate in determining what to do, instead of deciding it himself.

J.K. could have started the conference by saying: "Ralph, I want to get that Western Division really going, and I know you can do it. How do you feel about it, and what arrangements do you think would be best all around?"

Ralph would have answered frankly, and J.K. could have agreed, or could have negotiated some modifications. If Ralph had thus participated in setting up the arrangements, he would have been very strongly motivated to make them succeed. The situation was complex, and it would not have been easy for anyone *else* to figure out correctly, in advance, the arrangement best suited to motivate Ralph.

The best way to know how to motivate someone else is to check with them. There are a thousand ways to do it, but if it isn't done at all, the odds in favor of effective motivation go down—sometimes to quite an unfavorable long-shot.

3

MOTIVATIONAL LEVERAGE: HOW TO PUT FIVE BIG BASIC MOTIVATORS TO WORK FOR YOU

While each person is different from all other persons, there are a few very basic motivations that apply to all of us, though the degree to which they may apply, and the ways in which they may apply will vary greatly.

This chapter tells about five very important kinds of motivation, as originally developed by the great social scientist, Abraham Maslow.

1. MAKING FULL USE OF PHYSICAL MOTIVATORS IN HANDLING OTHERS

When we think about the motivations of others, it is necessary to be extremely open minded. People are motivated by all sorts of considerations, some of which may seem ridiculous, inadequate, shameful or even incredible to others.

Here is a blind girl who wants to become a lawyer; and here is a bright young lad who "cops out" on drugs. Here is someone scrimping and saving and "doing without" in order to be able to buy a dune-buggy or a snowmobile; and here is someone else motivated to use all his resources—even stealing—to impress a woman, or to gamble with strangers or to give his children an education. Here is someone making every effort and spending every waking moment practicing to become a professional musician, let us say; and here is someone else who would rather enjoy recreational activities than take advantage of a company training program. Here is a junior executive strongly motivated to become a more important member of the management team; and here is another who changes jobs to cut down on his commuting time so he can play tennis.

How to Understand What Is Motivating Someone

If you really want to know about another person's motivations, find out what brings him his really important satisfactions. Just observing what a person does may not tell you very much about why he does it. But learning about the way a person "gets his kicks" will tell you a lot—maybe all you need to know—about the whs of what he does.

Figure it this way: a person needs a good reason to make an effort. If you only observe him making the effort, you may not be able to tell what the reason is, why he does it. But if you see him show the signs of success, of achievement, of goal attainment, then you have good reason to know that he has got what he wanted. And if you know what he got, then you know what he wanted and thus why he *really* did what he did.

It is as if you see someone carefully and persistently saving every penny he can—"doing without," depriving himself, and putting the money in the bank. You don't know why—you don't know what he is saving for, or even if he is just habitually frugal. Then one day you learn that he has married, or made a down-payment on a house, or bought a car, or taken a long trip, or had done something else that usually takes quite a bit of money—and then at last you realize just what it was he was saving for. You learn the real motivation for all that painful economy.

Of course, it is possible to understand another person's motivation without waiting to see just what provides them with the basis for satisfaction. Sometimes they tell you, in a way that is quite convincing. Sometimes you can infer it rather accurately from what they are doing, or the way they do it. But if there is doubt, or if you really want to gain a more complete and certain understanding of another person's motivation, be sure to observe the satisfactions their motivations bring them, or, conversely, what it is they are trying to avoid or overcome.

The number of things that can motivate people is infinite, if we try to count the specific objectives of each individual. We call these *incentives*. We need to understand the general principles that govern or explain motivation by different incentives; the fundamental *needs* or drives or desires that lie behind the many, many specifics.

Recognizing the Patterns that Come from Physical Sources

Our basic motivations begin with our basic *needs* for such fundamentals as survival, and factors or considerations that are primarily physical. This includes physical security, and other physical factors, including the basic necessities of life. If we (or our families) seem to be in real danger, or if we need food or shelter or other necessities, then surely we are strongly motivated to do something about it. This is a powerful motivation, and we never lose it, no matter how well we succeed, and do not need it.

Physical security is, perhaps, not a common or obvious factor in most of our lives, but it does exist and it is important. When it bears upon us, it can be overwhelmingly motivational. Bullies know this; and some overbearing, aggressive people even habitually use or imply threats of physical violence to motivate others. Certain people seem to have an overwhelming physical presence; people are literally afraid to displease them. This often has the entirely negative effect of motivating people to avoid them.

Of course, people do vary greatly in their sensitivity to conditions in the physical environment, and the environment presents many factors that can greatly affect motivation. Physical comfort is a basic factor that can be very important. A room that is too cold, too draughty or too hot, can greatly reduce motivation and lower the quality of performance. Too much noise, too much distracting movement, inadequate or improper lighting, unsuitable chairs and desks, and other such inadequacies will have substantially adverse effects. It is quite worth while to evaluate the significant factors in the physical environment when considering motivational aspects of performance. Removing adverse environmental factors can have a positively motivating effect.

Changing People's Patterns of Living

People form habits, and habits resist change. Many habits have a physical basis. For instance, people are usually set in their own living patterns, schedules and routines. Most of them become used to leaving home at a regular time, travelling to work in a regular way, eating regular meals at regular times, and going to bed at a regular hour. They even get used to performing certain tasks in a certain way; and they fall into regular patterns in minor as well as major matters.

Working *WITH* Some Powerful Forces

When it is necessary to introduce change into such patterns, it is far better to motivate people to change, themselves, rather than to force changes upon them. Behavioral changes imposed from the outside are likely to be resisted. Try to motivate acceptance of change—even a welcoming—by explaining the reasons and by pointing out the advantages to those affected. Of course, the effect of this will depend on what advantages there are, and how advantageous they appear to the ones who have to make the changes.

Knowing the Far-Reaching Effects of Simple but Basic Factors

A simple, basic physical condition like fatigue can make an enormous difference in motivation and in performance. A salesman who is tired hates to make that last call, and probably will not handle it well. A weary clerk doesn't want to keep going at an exacting task, and is more likely to make mistakes. A tired workman does sloppier work. A tired supervisor becomes impatient, and may impair long-built-up relationships with the employees. A tired shop-steward will be less patient, less tolerant, less constructive in his attitude toward possible grievances. And so it goes. If you want to motivate a person to perform better, more, or differently, pick a time when they are rested, alert, and receptive; not when they are fatigued, and so interested only in resting.

Hunger is another basic factor that is often ignored, but can make quite a difference. Some people seem to change character when they are hungry—and not for the better. You are far more likely to get a good reception after lunch than just before. Most salesmen greatly prefer to see a prospect after he has "dined well";

the hungry prospect can be unusually negative (unless you are about to feed him).

Always consider the basic, physical factors in any situation. The basic needs are never absent, and may—at any time—be very important.

2. HARNESSING THE GREAT NEED THAT CAN WORK AGAINST YOU

Joe W. has heard rumors that the company he works for is losing money, that there may be some cutting back and some people may be let go. He is worried. His immediate superior and he do not get along very well. Joe has a wife and four children, he has to spend every nickel he earns, and he hasn't very much to fall back on. And Joe is almost fifty—another job will not be easy for him to come by.

Joe is greatly motivated to keep his job. This will show in his behavior: he is never late or absent now; he works harder than ever; he shows much greater willingness and eagerness, much more interest; he does all he can to prove to his boss how valuable he is, and to try to make his boss like him and appreciate him. His supervisor is impressed with Joe's seriousness and eagerness to please. Joe used to be more relaxed, more easy-going. Now he is really buckling down to his job.

One of Joe's ancestors, a few thousand years ago, had to run real hard to get away from a sabre-tooth tiger. Joe feels like he is in that same kind of fix now—but now he is running to escape the disaster of unemployment—and that looks pretty sabre-toothed to him. The need for economic security is driving Joe now—he needs a steady income in order to be confident that his and his family's basic needs will be taken care of.

If you want to motivate Joe, right now the best way would be to show him that whatever you want him to do will somehow be favorable to his economic security. That has the highest priority with Joe. And so it has with a lot of other people, even when their security is not really in danger. They often go on behaving the way they learned to behave when they were under the influence of the powerful motivation, self-preservation (economic or otherwise), even when that motivation has no longer any real application to them.

For instance, it has been noted that many of those who have survived concentration camps or prisoner-of-war camps, or who had other painful experiences of near-starvation, are likely to pile up food on their plates even now, as if they didn't know when they'd get another mouthful. Habits and attitudes formed under powerful motivations have a way of hanging on.

Joe isn't hungry yet, and he may never be; but he is driven by a great need to be sure that he and his family will never, ever be hungry—for sure! For Joe, that means holding his job.

How Insecurity Improves Some Behavior

Long ago, the principal motivation that most people had was to work hard to try to keep their jobs. There was a lot of unemployment, and there was no government-provided relief. Losing your job was a true disaster, and many employees lived in dread of that happening. Employers used the threat of discharge to drive employees into putting up with all sorts of conditions that would never be tolerated today, and most employees just gritted their teeth and worked all the harder. The alternative was all too unacceptable.

In many parts of the world, and even in some places in the United States, some of this still goes on. But the general trend is the other way. It won't go down with the competent worker who believes he can get another job; or with the irresponsible employee who counts on going (back) on relief; or with a member of an effective labor union, etc. Therefore the threat of unemployment falls heaviest on those who have reason to believe they would have difficulty finding another job or a job as good as the one they have; and on those who could not be satisfied with life on relief, or with collecting their unemployment insurance.

How You Can Use Some People's Insecurity to Influence Them

Loss of one's job usually involves some undesirable consequences, even if one can get another that pays as well. Too many job changes hurt one's record, and often have an effect on future employment and careers. There is the loss of pay until the new job starts. There is the change of routine, often involving more daily travel. There is the break with one's familiar fellow-workers; and there is the transitional period of getting used to the new ones. There is the insecurity of the new breaking-in period; and there is always the chance that the new job will turn out to be no more desirable than the old one. Differing chances of advancement, and loss of pension rights and other "fringe benefits" may make the change disadvantageous.

And so it goes, so that even those who do not fear economic insecurity may fear job insecurity as such. For them, the Motivational Leverage is similar to but not as strong as that of economic insecurity.

Using the Potent Lever of Dependence

"If you don't like it here, you don't have to stay" can push many into tolerating the extremely disagreeable. "That's what you're paid for!" and "You'll just have to measure up!" can force an employee to consider the alternatives, which may be even less acceptable. "Your work has been unsatisfactory—I won't warn you again!" will compel the addressee to decide if he would rather make the extra efforts required—or risk the consequences of not doing so (or quit).

Every employment situation carries within its nature the elements of potential motivation based on negative economic or other considerations; some, of course, far more than others. At the other end of the scale we find the employee who can motivate his employer by threatening to quit. The slow-down, the walk-out, the strike and the boycott are extensions of this bilateral economic relationship which must hold, by its very character, the varying possibilities of motivational pressure by one party upon the other. As long as any two people depend upon one another for a common economic purpose, one party can bring some sort of economic motivation to bear upon the other, according to the degree of dependence.

It is traditional to take advantage of the dependence of others in order to motivate them, even contrary to their inclinations. Parents have long used the economic dependence of children in order to control them; but such control is often resisted, and it is usually rejected as soon as the child can end the dependency. Meanwhile, the child is likely to be surly and resentful, and to yield to the economic control no more than is absolutely unavoidable. The employer's use of employee dependence is somewhat parallel, but there is nothing here resembling the family nurturing relationship, and so the resistance and resentment are likely to be bitter. Much more can be accomplished, motivationally, in other ways.

How to Build Up Others' Confidence in You

If you can measure what another person does, you may be able to hold them to a certain level of performance by motivating them, through their basic physical needs or through their economic dependence on you, to deliver the performance you demand. But if you want more than can be actually measured, you will probably have to motivate them in some other way.

You can motivate someone to dig a ditch or chop wood by paying so much per unit of visible achievement. But if you are concerned with quality and skill and intelligence and initiative and other elements of performance that cannot readily be measured or seen, you will need to have the work done by someone who *wants* to do it well.

You will need someone who has self-confidence; who feels secure enough to concentrate on exacting tasks and to derive satisfaction from doing a good job—and not just because they have no acceptable alternative.

You will need to motivate by reward instead of by punishment (deprivation) or by threat of punishment; you will need to be positive instead of negative in your attitude toward that person in order to motivate positive instead of negative attitudes in him.

In short, you will have to use basic needs and economic considerations in a positive way, and you will have to use motivational forces that are of a much higher order than these.

We discuss such motivational forces below.

3. BUILDING ON PEOPLE'S NEED
TO BE ACCEPTED

One of the most important basic motivations is *social*. Most of us don't like to be alone very long; perhaps all of us get lonesome rather easily. And when we are with others we want to be *accepted*—not rejected—by them. We like to feel welcome—even wanted; to have friends that really like us. When we feel that someone likes us, we may feel a warm glow of satisfaction. On the other hand, when we are conscious of being disliked or rejected, it usually bothers us. When we walk into our own homes, or the office, or when we visit someone or meet someone, the way we are received has a very real effect on us. All of us have a need which motivates us to be accepted, to be welcome, to be liked—a powerful need indeed.

This basic motivation leads us to do all sorts of things, from entertaining or giving gifts (for business or personal reasons) to being polite, telling jokes, contributing money or time and effort to causes, or by otherwise acting in such a way as to be "one of the gang," part of the group, "a member of the team," or otherwise consciously accepted as a regular component of an identifiable grouping. Just think how often you really make an effort to be liked, to be charming, to make a favorable impression.

Understanding How People Need Acceptance by Others

The need to be accepted leads people to do things they would never do otherwise. How often do ladies join bridge clubs, for instance, not because they really want to play bridge all that much, but really just to be accepted as a member of the group? In the same way, people in offices and factories often join bowling leagues, and enter into all sorts of other activities not only to participate in the particular activity around which the group is formed, but primarily to become associated with and accepted by the others.

Furthermore, when a group exists—however arbitrarily it may have been put together—the members usually have a special sense of coherence, of membership, of belonging—as against any other group. Employees who happen to be working together in a particular section of an office or part of a factory feel some kind of linkage that is different from what they feel even toward individuals they may know just as well or even better, but who are outside their work group.

The force that makes the individual want to be accepted is usually seen most clearly with children, who often suffer intensely when they feel rejected by their classmates or by the neighborhood "gang." Later, as in college, acceptance or rejection by a desired fraternity or sorority, or even by a recognized "circle," can make a tremendous difference in satisfaction or frustration. Even your very successful executive may feel that he has not really won true recognition until he has been accepted for membership in some prestigious club.

Applying the Powerful *Lever* of Social Needs

This great need to be accepted is such a potent motivator that you can use it in many ways to produce desired behavior in others. Since their social needs and goals often lead people to make financial sacrifices, to endure all sorts of initiation experiences, and even to change their way of life, we must realize that we, too, can bring about important results if we can harness the social needs of people to our purpose.

In its simplest form, this is done by granting or withholding your acceptance of a person to a greater degree of closeness to you or to your circle; by showing or refraining from showing various degrees of acceptance of a person. If the person wants to be accepted by you to a greater degree, or if a person really wants your friendship, then he will be motivated to act in a way he believes will bring about your acceptance of or friendliness to him. From this it is clear that the power of this lever depends on the value, to others, of acceptance by or friendship with *you*.

Making People Want to Be Accepted by You

Acceptance does not have to be awarded on a purely personal basis; it can be made to depend on an objective standard. A teacher may show special warmth to pupils who earn high grades; this will motivate some pupils to study harder. A headwaiter may show special favor to patrons who tip well; other patrons who want to be well-received by him learn to do likewise. A salesman may shower entertainment on "big" customers; this can undoubtedly influence some buyers' purchases.

An office manager may regulate the warmth of his contacts to match the quality of individual performance; this can motivate some employees to try harder. A foreman may show his appreciation of good work by greater friendliness; this can motivate some workers to improve their contribution. And so it goes.

Of course, for your acceptance of a person to have a motivational effect, it must have value for him. This value can be due to your position, your personality, or both.

Some people can accomplish a great deal on personality alone—somehow, people really want to feel "accepted" by them, to feel their friendliness. This may come about for a variety of reasons, depending on the kinds of "values" people are moved by.

It is important to understand the kind of motivation you want to exert—exactly what your *motivation plan* should accomplish. Then you work on building up your *standing* in the appropriate area.

Standing can be of many kinds. For instance, if you are a sloppy dresser, you will not have careful dressers seeking your approval of their clothing; and if dressing is really important to a person, a sloppy dresser will be more or less handicapped in any attempt to motivate them. You generally need *standing* that bears some relation to your *target plan*. But a strong personality can surmount such difficulties—people *want* the acceptance and friendship of those they respect.

There is also the power of the group: where a group exists, it can exert great motivational force on its members and on those who seek to join it. Sometimes this force is very strong, and a member of the group will act to conform to group pressure, even when he feels great reluctance to do what is required.

How a Bank Manager Used Social Leverage

Sylvia and Celia D., sisters, were both tellers in a bank branch, and they had gotten into the habit of coming to work well after the 8:30 A.M. opening. The manager, Otis F., had spoken to them about it repeatedly, but with little effect. Finally he decided to exploit social leverage to overcome their tardiness.

When the branch opened at 8:30, there was usually a rush of customers waiting to get cash for the day. Many of them would be waiting outside for the bank to open.

Otis saw, of course, that with the two windows of the sisters closed, the lines were longer at the other window, and so the other tellers had a lot more work. He also saw that he could use these conditions to bring social pressure to bear.

One morning when the sisters were late as usual, and the lines at the other tellers' windows were especially long, Otis walked along behind the counter. He stepped alongside each busy teller, in turn, and made comments like: "Too bad the sisters aren't here —again!" or "Your line would be a lot shorter if Sylvia and Celia were here!" or even "How much extra work do you suppose you have because those two girls are always late?"

The tellers, as a group, needed little more than this to find their own common cause against their absent colleagues. When the girls finally did show up, the other tellers made them understand, in no uncertain terms, that they were being unfair to their co-workers, and that such conduct was condemned. When lunch-time came, the two were left severely alone. Of course, they keenly felt the social pressure. Needing and wanting to be accepted by and to be friends with their fellow-workers—if not their boss—they did what was necessary.

Otis did not have to fire the two sisters, or even threaten to do so. He used effective social *leverage* on their social needs to motivate them to do as he wanted them to do.

4. TAKING ADVANTAGE OF THE DESIRE FOR STATUS

After people have more or less satisfied their basic needs for economic and other security, and their social needs for acceptance by the community and by the work-force at the plant, office or shop, they usually begin to feel another need—the need for some kind of status. This means that they want to be not only accepted, but also respected, approved, recognized as unique individuals—and, perhaps, even as being somewhat special.

Beyond the purely social motivation for acceptance we find the motivation to win *status*—the desire to be admired, to be looked up to; to be, in some way, "special." Some people even want to be envied.

People, of course, have developed innumerable kinds and signs of status, and also of ways for seeking these. Status sometimes represents an extension or exaggeration of more elementary goals. The seeking of money for necessities, comforts, or security becomes the seeking of wealth far beyond the needs even for luxurious self indulgence, and ostentation of such wealth. The desire to "belong" is translated into the ambition to be accepted in more and more exclusive circles, to become a member of elite groups, to move among the famous, the privileged, the distinguished, the great.

Of course, status is also won by achievement, by the attainment of leadership positions, or by the winning of conspicuous success in any field of endeavor, from Little League Baseball through collegiate wrestling to starring on one's own "hour" on the TV, etc. And status is manifested by popularity, by wealth and possessions, by positions and titles, by the recognition of others, by the exercise of authority or influence, by visible accomplishment, etc.

The need for status is shown in many ways. Some people dress to make an impression; others are purposely careless to show they really don't care about making an impression that way.

Some people boast about their cars, or their houses, or their children; or about relatives or ancestors that have perhaps achieved some distinction; or about their education, etc. Others are "name-droppers"—they like to mention the names of well-known people—"personalities"—they have somehow met or had some connection with—however fleeting and insignificant the contact may have been. Some people even like to show or tell you how much money they have or spend.

How to Recognize the Desire for Status

Some people talk about their better golf scores, the fish they have caught, the slopes they have skied, the places they have travelled to, the antiques they have collected, the games they have won, the sports events they have witnessed.

Many like to impress you with their own ego-satisfying triumphs—their promotions, their business successes, even the arguments they have won, the sales they have clinched, the deals they have made, the clever remarks or "comebacks" or "put-downs" they have thought up; the shrewd decisions, the being "right," the correctness of their predictions, and many other ways of trying to make other people think they are as good as or better than they think they are themselves.

All of this means they are seeking *status*. This is one of the most common forms of behavior, and it offers you excellent opportunities to influence or persuade people. When you understand people's seeking for status, you have one of the most common and best bases for motivating them.

Understanding the Different Kinds of Status that People Want

If you are going to motivate someone, one of the most useful things you can do is to know if they are seeking any kind or kinds of status, and to arrive at an understanding of just what kind of status they are seeking. This is usually easy to do if you listen to them carefully and then ask yourself these two questions:

A. What kind of an impression is he (she) trying to make on me?
B. Why?

If you can give yourself good answers to these two questions —which should be easy—then you are already well on the way toward having the insights that should enable you to make a sound *motivation plan* to use on that *motivation target*, based upon the kind of status they are seeking.

How You Can Use People's Desire for Status to Influence Them

Many people seek the kind of status that comes from a formal or official position, like being an officer in the Armed Forces, or a manager or executive in a corporation, or an official of a society or association. If so, you can probably think of a way to help them to gain such a position, or to succeed or look well in such a position if they are already in it.

If you yourself are not in a position to appoint them or even nominate them, you can usually "put in a good word" somewhere, make an informal suggestion, speak favorably about them to their boss, etc. In this way you can become a valuable supporter of their quest for status, and this can greatly improve your *standing* with them.

The whole activity is very much like that involving a politician seeking office: he needs all kinds of support, and can be greatly influenced by those who support him. And remember also that a title can confer status, whatever may or may not be behind it; and that many people are eager for status-conferring titles, and will do a lot to win them.

If the *target individual's* need for status is less specific, you can still focus on it and become an important *and influential* supporter. You know how people who have publicity agents are influenced by them—they advise on what will help or hurt the "image" they are trying to build.

If you understand the kind of status the *target individual* really wants, and show that you recognize this status, and believe he (she) really deserves such status, you can build your *standing* to become a valued part of the status itself. Then *your* admiration and *your* appreciation, together with *your* reinforcement, will put you in a most advantageous, influential position.

How You Can Create Desires for Status

Sometimes, of course, the *target individual* may not reveal any need for status that you feel you can work with. In such cases you can generally find a status goal for them that they will accept. You can express interest or admiration or encouragement for one or more of the *target individual's* qualities or capabilities or activities—or even hobbies—and thus stimulate them to a more active sense of the status or potential status involved. In fact, you may be especially identified with the status that is the subject of this new need, and in this way you can be especially influential.

How Tony G. Created and Then Benefited by a Colleague's Desire for Status

Tony G. was foreman of a large auto repair shop. He was highly dependent upon the willing cooperation of the supervisor of the Spare Parts Department—a position that was about to become vacant because of the impending retirement of the occupant.

The obvious successor was a senior inventory clerk with whom Tony had had repeated difficulties. He dreaded the day when this man would become supervisor of the Spare Parts Department.

There was another man in the Spare Parts Department who was always very cooperative—Ben Z., the "number two man," in charge of the counter. Tony invited Ben to lunch, and sounded him out on the idea of *his* becoming supervisor of the department.

"Gee—I never thought of that! Do you think I have a chance?" Ben responded. "Wouldn't that be something!"

"Of course you have a chance—a good chance," Tony encouraged. "I'll speak to the manager about it this afternoon, and recommend you to him. We'll talk to the owner, and his son, too; and you better write up your record, and emphasize your experience, and all the nice things people have said about your service at the counter. I believe we might even get your boss to recommend you, or at least to mention you favorably as a possibility, before he retires.''

The result of this conversation was that Ben became more and more hungry for the status of supervisor, and so became more and more committed to seeking the position he had never thought about before Tony suggested it and offered to help. They put on a successful campaign; Ben got the promotion; and Tony had a grateful friend who ran the Spare Parts Department most cooperatively. And even if Ben had not finally been able to move into that spot, Tony would have been ahead: he would have been assured of a warm supporter in that department.

The drive for status is surely one of the most important influences at work on your friends, your neighbors, and the people you work for and with. You can easily harness that drive to influence people, and to put real power behind your *motivation plan*.

5. RIDING THE DRIVE THAT GOES ON GETTING WONDERFUL RESULTS

There is another kind of motivation that is more important than most people realize. This is when a person feels that he has certain abilities, potentials, talents—and that he wants to have the satisfaction of realizing and fulfilling these by ''doing his thing.'' Sometimes called ''self-fulfillment'' or ''self-actualization,'' this kind of motivation can be extremely strong, especially in individuals who seek seriously to develop or build their personal capabilities, or to use these to the fullest.

Creative people, whether artistic or scientific, are motivated by the desire to create, to discover, to add to human knowledge or understanding or insight or enjoyment. They often devote themselves to such goals, even with little or no regard for such motivations as security, acceptance or status. People who are extremely public-spirited, or so dedicated to special causes that they give themselves unstintingly—''unselfishly''—these also seem to disregard, largely or completely, the motivations for security, acceptance and status.

Some people actually reject opportunities for which others would sacrifice a great deal, solely in order to do what they have decided is "right" for them—regardless of security, acceptance, or status. Some do this even when it means poverty, the disapproval of others or even rejection by friends and family. And what of those who willingly risk their lives from a sense of duty?

The Powerful Drive that Takes Many Forms

Alan M. showed a need for something beyond money, social acceptance and status when he quit a successful career as a pharmacist to go to Uganda with the Youth Corps. But Patricia D. also showed a certain drive for self-actualization when she quit a well-paying job typing scanner sheets for a bank's computer because it did not utilize her skills in taking dictation and typing letters. Any person who wishes he had a "more interesting" or a "more satisfying" job is showing some of the effects of the drive for self-realization.

A person who wants to complete or enlarge his own education is motivated, at least in part, by this higher form of motivation, though the desire to make more money and the desire for status may also be involved.

Motivations are often—perhaps always—more or less combined. In fact, they are often in conflict. A person who needs a job is offered one that pays well, but is "undignified." If the motivation for security is stronger than that for status, he may accept it. If status is more of a motivation than security, he may reject it.

What *Really* Moved the New Branch Manager

Paul D., General Sales Manager of Southern Office Supply, was quite puzzled by his new Branch Manager, Larry G., in the Riverside Branch, whom Paul had hired on the basis of several strong references. Larry had run sales and service branches successfully for several companies before a reorganization had led him to seek employment with Paul's company.

It was clear that Larry was intelligent, experienced and capable. But he seemed to be a plodder. He was doing the job well enough to be kept on, but not as well as Paul had hoped. He seemed to be holding himself in, not to be making the effort he could make. Paul felt that if he only knew how, he ought to be able to get Larry moving faster and harder and better. This bothered Paul, and he kept thinking about this situation, and looking for some clue as to how he might be able to "light a fire" under Larry. Then, one happy day, the light dawned.

Paul was in his office, busy with his "incoming" basket, when his secretary came in to tell him that Larry was outside and wanted to see him. Paul had him come in immediately, wondering what had led to this un-routine visit. Larry came in, quiet, restrained, but also, it seemed, tense, and highly intent on whatever purpose it was that had brought him.

"Hello, Larry," Paul greeted him. "What's on your mind?" He waved at a chair.

Larry sat down, turned to Paul, and spoke very quietly.

"You remember telling me about that Castelli account?" Larry asked.

"Why, yes!" Paul replied. "I told you not to waste time on it, because we'd never get it."

"Well," Larry answered, very quietly, "We've got it."

Paul was greatly surprised, but, of course, extremely pleased at what was a really large piece of new business.

"Gee, that's wonderful, Larry," Paul told him, quite sincerely and without embarrassment at having been proved wrong. "Tell me about it."

Larry launched into an account of his triumph, but did it quite objectively, obviously restraining himself from crowing, or claiming any special credit. Yet it was clear from his story that he had been determined to land the Castelli account from the moment Paul had told him not to bother about it.

Larry had obviously taken Paul's negative advice as a very special *challenge*, in response to which he had put forth great efforts, careful planning, and the most serious and sustained effort. His success was a real mark of capability, since Paul knew that a Castelli nephew, who was with Paul's leading competitor, had had the inside track for supplying the furnishings and equipment for the big new Castelli department store.

Understanding the Drive that Motivates People in a Very Special Way

After Paul had listened to Larry's story, and had congratulated him and sent him back to his branch with warm commendations, he began to think about what had just happened. It was clear that Larry had been *highly* motivated to go after the Castelli account. He had been motivated to do this *in spite of* Paul's advice. Maybe—could it be?—he was motivated *because* of Paul's advice! The more Paul thought about it, the more he felt certain he had an important clue to Larry's motivation. Larry had really—obviously—taken *great satisfaction* in doing what Paul had said could not be done.

Now the question arose as to the precise nature of the motivation. Was it basically to show what he could really do? Or was it just to prove Paul wrong?

The Challenge: How You Can Influence People Through Their Ambitions

Paul checked back, in memory, over the significant elements in Larry's performance. Always, he had shown competence in, but little interest in routine; always he had shown great interest in problems, plans, difficulties, unfinished business. It was clear that Larry was not only motivated by challenges and difficulties, but he was determined to prove himself—to prove himself capable of accomplishing the exceptional. *He derived his satisfaction* from tackling and succeeding in challenges and problems; from *showing what he could do*—not in routine, regular, long-drawn out performances, but in clear-cut, dramatic situations, where success would stamp him as *unusual, exceptional,* even *distinguished*.

And Paul had been unable to perceive this triumph-seeking motivation until he observed the almost passionate satisfaction that had Larry almost trembling when he reported his surprising success with Castelli. It was the intensity of Larry's satisfaction that gave Paul the clue to Larry's real motivation. No one who saw how more-than-pleased he was with his achievement could doubt the intensity of the motivation that drove him to seek it.

How an Idea Can Shape a Life; and How *You* Can Shape the Idea

As satisfaction comes from the fulfillment of a need or want, so it offers the basic clue to the motivations that arise from our needs or wants. Larry wanted to prove to himself and to others what he could do. So he was motivated to seek and meet challenges. When he succeeded, he felt deep gratification. And that was observable, and so it revealed the motivation that gave rise to it. Paul was astute enough to know, when he noted Larry's great satisfaction, that he had—at last—the long-sought clue to motivating Larry.

Almost everyone worth motivating is seeking to be more of what he can be, than he is now. Almost everyone believes he could be, and do, more and better than he is or does. Almost everyone would like to feel that he is really using his potentials, and using them well, and using them for something worthwhile. Almost everyone is looking, hoping, for a chance to move in that direction, even though few people show it.

You can make a *motivation plan* that ties into this drive; you can challenge your *target individual* to show what he really can do, and you will be applying one of the most potent and effective ways of motivating people that anyone can use.

By offering challenges, you can help others to exert and apply their potentials to worthwhile goals that will bring them great and lasting satisfactions, and even change their lives for the better.

4

HOW TO ACTIVATE
OTHER POTENT HUMAN DRIVES TO
GAIN MOTIVATIONAL LEVERAGE

There are, of course, many different human drives that can exert strong motivational forces on different individuals under various conditions. This chapter discusses the most important of these, besides the five big ones considered in Chapter 3.

The needs, drives and wants discussed in Chapter 3 can, of course, be used to influence almost anyone for almost any reasonable purpose. But there are still other powerful motivating forces that may be even more appropriate for use with some people, and under some circumstances. We will discuss these in the first two sections of this chapter.

1. EXPLOITING THE FORCE THAT
DRIVES THE MOST INTELLIGENT

There is a drive that is so fundamental that you can see it at work almost any time, in the behavior of animals, as well as people. If you watch a dog sniffing to find out the meaning of a scent, or a cat exploring its environment, you will have a clue to an absolutely basic drive that leads to special, information-seeking behavior.

The psychological basis for this goes back to the days when man had to be alert to everything around him if he wanted to survive. He had to sniff the air, and listen, and look—or he might be surprised by a man-killing animal, or an enemy. This ancient necessity for survival has stayed with us in many forms, and shows itself today in extremes that range from the dedicated quest for new knowledge by the scientist and the scholar, to the idle curiosity of a neighborly housewife; from the trained investigation of skilled reporter or detective, to the readers of newspaper gossip columns.

People want to know; and the newspapers and news bulletins and the wealth of non-fiction books and articles in magazines show this, as does all educational activity, especially the whole range of voluntary participation by adults in all kinds of courses and training programs.

People want to know what is going on in their families and in their businesses and social organizations; in their neighborhoods; and in their special interest areas, such as politics, sports, "society," hobbies, fields of special knowledge or experience, etc. People like to know the prices of things, the ages of other people, a good movie to see, a good restaurant or night club to try, an attractive or inexpensive place to go during vacation, etc. Housewives welcome new recipes, new and better ways of carrying out household chores. Football fans and fans of other sports never tire of hearing the latest about their favorite teams and players, athletes and coaches—even horses and dogs.

There is no limit to the desire that people have to know, to learn, to find out. And you can use this very strong drive to bring success to your *motivation plan*.

How to Gain from Other People's Curiosity

When you select a *motivation target*, you must, of course, study that person's likes and dislikes, interests and desires. Study also the areas in which his interests especially lead him to seek and welcome news or information. If you can be the person who can tell him something he is glad to know, your *standing* will really grow.

If you can develop the ability to discuss his favorite subject with him, you will have a great *advantage*. But if you can add to his knowledge of that subject, you will have an even greater *advantage*. A common interest can do a lot for your *leverage*; but becoming a *resource* on the subject of common interest can do far more.

Frank S. was assistant manager of a department in a large office. In this position, he was usually among the first to "know what was going on" in that department. Many of the other employees sought him out, to learn as early as possible about changes and new developments. It soon became known that if you were "nice" to Frank, he would keep you posted, especially on matters that concerned you. This gave him quite a lot of *leverage,* not only in his department, but also outside it. He was able to use this to get himself promoted, to be full manager of another department.

Josh G. was a salesman in a firm that did many kinds of packaging. He made up his mind to study all the important aspects of the industry, and to keep up with developments. He read all the trade journals carefully, and kept a notebook on significant matters. It soon became known that Josh's own success was due to his special knowledge, and he was called upon to help the other salesmen with information affecting their accounts and territories. Soon the sales manager also began to tap Frank's fund of information, and soon after that Frank was made Assistant Sales Manager, and was next in line for the big job.

Similar was the example of young George G., who found his knowledge of optics so helpful. (See Chapter 2, Section 2.)

How to Get Ahead by Supplying What Others Want to Know

People talk about the subjects that interest them, whether they know much about them or not. Often, they reveal that they would like to know something, or know more about some subject. If you can then say something like: "Well, maybe I can help you out on that"—or "As it happens, I do know about that"—or "I happen to have quite a lot of information on that subject"—or "I've just been reading (or just made a study) about that"—or "I can find that out for you"—or use any other appropriate way of letting them know that you can make a contribution they will value, then your *standing* will grow—but fast!

There are two ways of going about the process of getting into this position. First, think clearly and objectively about the subject areas in which you now have a reasonably good foundation of knowledge. Which of these can be used, or can be developed to be used, as a source that will contribute noticeably to a field that is of genuine interest to a *target individual*, or, better yet, to the group of which the *target individual* is a member? If you can identify such a subject area, then you have a head start on your *motivation plan*.

If you cannot identify such a subject area within your present competence, then you must consider the feasibility of developing one. You may have to read, study, or even take courses. This may be a very worthwhile project that can help you in many different ways, apart from helping you with your *motivation plan*.

How to Build Interest that Will Help You Motivate

Harold S. wanted to be the junior executive who would be chosen to succeed his boss, Aaron T. But Harold had stiff competition from two other junior executives.

Harold knew that Mr. T.'s hobby was classical music: he was always going to operas, concerts and recitals. Neither of Harold's rivals was very knowledgeable about music, and neither was Harold. But Harold knew that Mr. T. believed the big job called for a cultured person, and to Mr. T., culture meant music.

So Harold decided to learn about classical music. He enrolled in a course in the University Extension; he subscribed for a concert series; he bought records and tapes; and he bought and read books on Wagner, Beethoven, Bach and Brahms, and even Vivaldi.

Harold didn't rush things, but one day he was able to ask Aaron T. how he had enjoyed the symphony concert the night before. Mr. T. was surprised, especially when Harold let him know he had been there. They began to discuss it, and Harold was able to quote from or refer to the reviews in that morning's papers, and even the past reviews of similar performances. Harold had really done his homework!

Mr. T. took in this information on his hobby, and he was both gratified and impressed. Harold's "image" had changed. He gained greatly in *standing*, and this undoubtedly helped him to get Mr. T.'s recommendation to succeed him, when Mr. T. retired the next year. And meanwhile, Harold really gained in another way—he greatly enjoyed his own new hobby.

How to Use Information to Influence People

People are influenced by what they know—or think they know—and by what they learn. And when people are interested or curious, they want to know more. If you have the information people need, they will turn to you. In any conference, committee meeting or group interchange, the man who gives others the impression of *KNOWING* is the one most likely to be listened to—and followed.

Pick your opportunities, and prepare yourself. Even one successful occasion, where everyone else can see that you are *prepared and informed,* can change your *standing* greatly, and enlarge your influence with people. Give it a good try. There is no better way to build *leverage* for future *motivation plans*.

2. CAPITALIZING ON THE POWER OF PREFERENCE

There are all sorts of proverbs and old sayings and bits of ancient wisdom that testify to the diversity and range of human tastes. "One man's meat is another's poison" expresses the idea very well. The Romans said: *De gustibus non disputandum est,* which means something like "It is useless to argue about individual taste."

Different people certainly value different things, and even people who value the same things often do so for different reasons. Objects of art may be appreciated for their beauty, or for their value. Politicians may be condemned or admired for the same act. Reviewers differ greatly in their reactions to plays, movies, ballets, art exhibitions, operas, concerts, etc. Journalists report the same events quite differently. Editorial writers take opposing sides on issues and developments. Members of a family often disagree about the way all sorts of things appear to them. And so it goes.

How to Be Aware of People's Likes and Dislikes

You can use people's likes and dislikes effectively to help you to motivate them. You can use these to gain *standing* and *advantage* and *leverage*; and so they should have an important place in most *motivation plans*.

But before you can use them, you have to know what they are.

You have to spot them, identify them, and understand them. You need to develop the ability to become quickly aware of the most significant likes and dislikes of the *target individual*.

You can do this—usually rather easily—by taking in and recognizing the significances of many of the actions and utterances of the *target individual*. People simply cannot help giving away their attitudes and feelings toward the things they talk about or do something about; and if you listen or observe carefully you can almost always pick out the areas and directions of preference. It is rare when people try to hide these, and even when they do, the truth usually comes through to the thoughtful observer or listener.

Recognizing Tastes, Preferences, Prejudices, Choices— and What This Can Do For You

Let's say Pete has invited his new boss, Joe, and his wife, to dinner in his home. Let us consider the possibilities of several different openings for an appropriate subject.

    A. "Joe—cocktails—what would you and Marian prefer?""Thanks, Pete, but neither Marian nor I ever drink cocktails."

An awkward moment—probably some loss of Pete's *standing*.

    B. "Marian has her cocktail, Joe; what would you like?" "Thanks, Pete—a Scotch on the Rocks, please."

That was all right perhaps; but compare it with C.

    C. "I know you like Scotch on the Rocks, Joe—right? Coming up!"

A shows a gross ignorance of the guests' prejudices, and probably would cause some embarrassment. How much better if Pete knew they were total abstainers—he could have avoided the whole problem. Better, he could have shown his understanding and consideration by offering a soft drink.

B offers hospitality that is accepted; but by having to ask what his guest wanted, Pete demonstrated that he did not know—a confirmation of their superficial acquaintance.

In *C*, however, Pete showed not only that he knew his guests' taste in cocktails, but also that it was not the first time he had a drink with Joe; and furthermore that he was interested enough to remember this preference from previous experience—perhaps an office party.

Truly, *C* could help Pete's *standing* with Joe more than *B*, and far more than *A*. Joe might not be acutely conscious of the difference, but it would surely affect his overall impression of his first visit to Pete's home.

Understanding the Intangibles that Are So Important to People

It is easy to understand when someone wants a car, a new fur coat, a boat, a country place, a hi-fi set, or any other tangible, visible, usable thing. But people often forget that another person may feel just as strongly, or even more so, about *intangibles*—not so much *things* as *special satisfactions*.

Many a woman—even nowadays—has a soft spot in her heart for the man who never fails to light her cigarette, stand up when she enters or leaves, and otherwise observes the old-fashioned courtesies that used to carry the message of respect, of special recognition of a woman's privileged position as a "lady."

Many a person feels a special appreciation for an apt quotation from classical literature or from history, or for a stimulating invocation of some appropriate cultural reference. Some people are greatly pleased when they hear another give expression to an idea that is highly artistic, or impressively ethical, or convincingly logical, or highly innovative, or unusually challenging, or especially enlightening or insightful, or otherwise particularly interesting.

You can build all kinds of valuable *standing* by gratifying such tastes as these; and if you have an aptitude for any of them, you can build it into a substantial *advantage* with people who are particularly inclined to appreciate and value such contributions.

Be alert to expressions of appreciation or admiration as clues that such tastes for intangibles exist, and as to what will gratify them. Study and remember the incidents when your *target individual* has been moved by an intangible—especially of a kind that you might provide. There are few better ways to build *standing*.

Using People's Likes and Dislikes to Influence Them

You can gain valuable *leverage* by using the positive *likes* (and, of course, avoiding the *dislikes*) of your *target individual*, when it comes to persuading or influencing him. For instance, if you are recommending a certain business plan, be sure of the musical tastes of your *target individual* before you assure him that it will move along like a Bach fugue—or a ballad.

An advertising account executive was surprised when he had a series of ad illustrations cancelled after he told the president of the client company that they were "like Picasso." But he got quick approval of a batch of radio commercials (for a different client) when he described the music as being "in the same spirit as the Beatles."

Believe it or not, orders have been lost because salesmen entertained customers at musicals their wives considered "in poor taste"; and orders have been won because the salesman exchanged appreciative comments with the prospect or his wife on certain features of architecture, industrial design or even sunsets.

People like to be reminded of the things they like, and they tend to react favorably to anything that is associated with the things they like. If you want to influence them, this tendency provides one of your great opportunities to build *standing*, develop *advantages*, and apply stronger *leverage*, by building your identification with the intangibles that your *target individual* likes.

3. ENLISTING ANOTHER'S SELF-IMAGE IN YOUR CAUSE

Most people who have thought about the subject seriously, agree that language is one kind of "thing," and reality is quite another kind; and that, no matter how hard we try, it is difficult if not impossible to get an exact correspondence between reality and language. In addition, people "see" things differently from one another, and from reality; and the "reality" they may seek to express can only be the "reality" *they* "see"—which may differ from the "reality" you or I would see.

And there is still another difficulty, in that people often are not really trying to communicate even their own "reality" exactly. They do not always tell what they know; they do not always "tell it like it is"; and they often say what they have to say with a strong "slant"—aimed at getting you to "see it their way," to be persuaded to their attitude or point of view. And, finally, what we hear gives us impressions and conveys ideas or images that may be quite different from those that are intended, due to our own individual way of reacting to the words and tone of voice and gestures and other elements of the total communication effect.

When you take all of this into consideration, it is easy to see that we should be careful not to assume that we understand a person's motivations until we have sufficient evidence to go on, and have been able to check our impressions to be reasonably sure.

The Self-Image, and How It Shows Itself

One of the best ways to understnad people's motivations is to understand how they "see" themselves: the image of themselves that lies, for them, behind their words and acts. For each of us has a "self-concept" or "self-image": we picture ourselves to ourselves, and this picture is different from the picture anyone else can have of us. When our self-image is fairly realistic, other people come closer to seeing us as we see ourselves; but when there is a big difference between our self-image and the way we appear to others, then some of the things we do or say are likely to bring out such remarks as: "WHO does he think he IS?"

What Someone's Self-Image Can Mean to You

The manager of a large office was startled, one morning, when a very new employee, a youngster just three months out of high school, and with less than that much "experience," asked for an interview, and then demanded that he be considered for a supervisory position. His self-image made him seem a candidate for supervisor—in his own eyes. This was so far from the image of him then held by the manager that the episode seemed bizarre; the lad was regarded as ridiculously, unrealistically presumptuous. His motivation was clear, but it bore no relation to his real *standing*; and he had no *advantage* working for him. The manager had no motivation to offer him even a minor promotion. (But the manager was motivated to keep an eye on him.)

How the Self-Image Influences the Way People Act

In that same office, when an opening for supervisor did occur, the manager called in a middle-aged clerk, Arnie T., and offered him the post. Arnie was surprised and overwhelmed. He had been in one job over ten years, had adjusted to that situation, and had pretty well lost any idea of moving up. He saw himself as a clerk; his self-image was a modest one.

The youngster's self-image led him to act aggressively to try to make it real. Arnie's self-image led him to relax and adjust. If you understood those two self-images—the way those two saw themselves—you would certainly be helped to understand better why they acted and talked and behaved as they did; and you would have a sort of window on their motivations.

The individual's self-image is a reflection of his motivations, needs, personality, etc., and in return, it influences the individual's behavior, and thus suggests a kind of subjective evaluation of the motivations.

For instance: the youngster referred to above was motivated to become a supervisor. All well and good, but in his own self-image, he already felt himself to be qualified to *be* a supervisor, *now*. *That* was not realistic; and the fact that he felt that way would make the manager doubt him and his judgment, especially when the lad was judging himself.

If and when that youngster ever becomes a supervisor, he can be expected to act aggressively, "un-self-doubtingly," super-confidently—to be "a mover and a shaker." Some, at least, of the people he supervises then will resent him severely. But if his judgment and his ability to deal with others should match his other very positive characteristics, then he might go far. If not, he might cause more trouble than he would be worth, as a supervisor.

On the other hand, old Arnie had not really thought of himself as a possible supervisor for a long time. It was apparent that his own self-image was not a very flattering one. Arnie's motivation would still be to adjust; and the manager would, hopefully, put him in a spot where maintaining the *status quo* would be more important than changing it, or than dealing with troublesome problems involving people.

Acts that Give Away a Self-Image

It is sometimes easy to understand another person's self-image, especially when they talk about themselves, or even when they talk about other people. When they comment on or pass judgment on other people, they are saying something about themselves.

Peter D. is the head of the Order Department for a large wholesaler. Here are some of his frequent comments on some of the salesmen:

"That young idiot Red thinks he knows it all. I told him Armstrong's always want their shipments in 1000 lb. lots, but, of course, he wouldn't listen."

"If it wasn't for the way this department edits the orders the salesmen send in, we'd be in an even worse mess."

"Greg N. is the only one of the salesmen who really knows how to handle an order."

"I'd like to be in Arthur S.'s place for just *one* week. *I'd* get some of these things straightened out." (Arthur S. is the sales manager.)

"I've set up the best procedures. It's just as easy to handle an order properly as it is to foul it up and cause a lot of trouble. Why don't they do it? Greg is the only one who does."

How a Salesman Came to Understand a Department Head

To most of the salesmen, Peter D. is an old sour-puss; a nuisance who makes a big fuss, and bothers everybody over ridiculous procedural details. But Greg N., one of the more perceptive salesmen, has a somewhat different view.

"You have to understand Peter," he explains to a colleague, "and then you can get along with him fine. After all, *he's* in charge of Order Processing. If that isn't important, he isn't important. He thinks it's *very* important; and if you think about it, you have to admit it has to be done; and if it isn't done well it can louse us up real good; and it has to start with the orders and the instructions that we write.

"The only trouble with Pete, really, is that he is determined to do a truly perfect job of order processing, no less; he's practically obsessed with it. And that's good. All we have to do, really, is play along. I go see him every now and then, and ask his advice about how to write up an order, when there's any doubt. He likes that, and he'll do anything to be helpful, if you ask him. Then he gives you credit for being cooperative, and trying to follow the procedures he set up. It's so easy to play it his way—and it pays!"

Greg has been able to understand that the motivations affecting Peter D.'s behavior toward the salesmen are of several kinds: *self-fulfillment* (he wants to run the best possible Order Processing Department); *status* (he wants to be recognized as *the* authority on procedures relating to orders; and *acceptance* (he wants to be accepted as a friendly, helpful fellow-worker—but only on his own terms).

Greg has used his understanding of Peter's motivations to win his help and support, and even his praise. All of this helps to make Greg a more likely candidate than the other salesmen for taking over Arthur S.'s post as sales manager, when Arthur retires.

4. EXPOSING THE REAL MOTIVATION BEHIND "THE MOTIVATION"

In the preceding chapter we discussed some basic motivations, especially those for security, social acceptance, status and self-fulfillment. If you keep these four in mind and understand them and how they can influence behavior, you will find that almost all the *specific* motivations you can uncover can fit into one or another of these, or some combination of these.

If a person's behavior reveals a specific goal, we can try to relate it to one of these four basic motivations. For instance: an executive demands an increase in salary. He is probably not insecure, or he would not make such a demand. Is he concerned about acceptance? Perhaps. Demanding a raise is one way of finding out just how "accepted" he really is. Or is it a matter of status? Can it be that he wants to make sure he is better paid than his apparent peers? And then, can the demand be related to self-fulfillment? Is it part of a plan to achieve some highly personal goal that is not motivated primarily by the needs for security, acceptance, or status?

Spotting the Causes Behind the Reasons, So You Can Deal with Them

It may be important to know more about this executive's motivations than simply that he wants a higher salary. If that is all he wants, and he is feeling quite secure, it may mean that he has a pretty good offer from some other company, and he is checking to see if that offer will be matched or bettered. Or—is he bluffing? Just how secure does he really feel? Some people always act with what seems to be great self-assurance; others always seem hesitant, diffident, cautious, unsure. Yet a person of the first kind may be a big "phoney"; and one of the second kind may be, in fact, supremely confident.

You have to check it out against performance. *WHY* does he

want a higher salary? Is it because he really needs or wants the money? Or is it for some other reason? For instance:

1. His wife may have urged and pestered him into demanding a raise.
2. One or more of his outside friends may have received a big raise.
3. Someone may have been telling him he should be getting more.
4. He may be comparing himself to some other executives who are—or who he believes are—receiving higher salaries.

How You Can Analyze Actions Systematically

On the other hand, he may not really need or especially want the money, as such, but he values it for its "symbol value."

5. Higher pay would be proof that he is more highly valued—("accepted").
6. Higher pay means higher status:
    a. In the company.
    b. At home.
    c. Among his friends.
    d. Among his professional colleagues in other companies.
7. Higher pay *now* means he can demand still higher pay if he leaves to work for another employer.
8. Higher pay may lead to a new title—more status.
9. Higher status could make it easier to do more of what he wants to do; to make a more distinctively personal contribution; to enjoy more, or come closer to "self-fulfillment."

And of course there can be many other reasons.

If *you* have to make a recommendation or a decision about this executive's demand, it would certainly help if you knew the real *why*—the *kind* of motivation behind the executive's act. Without knowing this, really, your choice is to give him what he demands, or to refuse—and such a decision will probably be based on the company's needs or motivations alone. You might lose a good man unnecessarily, or alienate a good man into deleterious resentment.

How to Look for the Motivation Behind "The Motivation"

How can you tell the motivation that is really behind the apparent motivation?

The best way—really the only way—is to recognize that you must try to observe on three levels: what he says; what he does; and *WHY*. *WHY* is what you want to know: that clues you to the motivation. What he says, you can hear (by what he says in your hearing) or have relayed to you (by those who hear it). What he does, you can observe directly, or infer from reports or results. The *WHY* you will have to figure out from what you hear and what you see; and so the more you hear and see, and the more carefully you listen and observe, the more reliably you can figure out the *WHY*.

In space, a point has no direction; it doesn't lead anywhere by itself; it can be the center of a circle (or sphere) of 360°; and from that one point you can go in any direction. But two points give you a straight line.

In the same way, if you hear one utterance, or observe one act, it is foolish to take this as a guideline to a person's nature, or a clear indication of his motivation. But if you hear several utterances and can find some connection—some significance in common, you can "draw a line" from one to another.

And so, if you observe or know of several different acts, you can usually find a direction from them. Best of all, if you can gather a consistent connection between words and deeds, you will have a very valuable pointer to that person's motivations. After all, some people turn out to be simpler, easier to "read" than others: they say what they think, and mean what they say. While others—at least part of the time—may try to say what they think you want (or ought) to hear. Make up your mind if words and deeds are consistent; if not, judge the motivations from what they do—not what they say.

What Norma B. *Did,* to Get What She Wanted

Norma B. was an account executive in a fast-growing advertising agency. She was excellent at her work, handled accounts well and was helpful toward new business. Yet she was a problem to the agency president, Neil R., because she kept saying she'd prefer to be a copywriter. He figured she was much more valuable to the agency as an account executive. And yet she kept coming up with these requests to be considered for the copy department.

Neil checked up on what she *did*, as well as on what she *said;* and he found out *WHY*. She didn't get along very well with the head of the copy department; she often criticized the copy they prepared for her accounts. The copy department, on the other hand, usually won out, through actual tests of the copy, or through account acceptance. Neil found that, each time this happened, Norma talked about becoming a copywriter. Now he had his line between what Norma *did* and what Norma *said*. And it pointed to the WHY: Norma talked as she did because her real motivation was to express her belief that she was very knowledgeable about writing copy—a logical tactic in her struggle with the copy department.

Now, was it for security, acceptance, status or self-fulfillment? Neil felt that Norma's position in the agency and with her accounts was rather secure; and that she had every reason to know this, and so to feel herself accepted in both areas. Then, was it status, or self-fulfillment? And if the motivation was primarily for status, was it for status as a copywriter? Or for status in her disputes with the copy department? How was Neil to know? Of course, his own motivation was to bring about better cooperation between Norma and the copy department. How could he motivate her in this direction?

The next time Norma expressed a wish to be a copywriter, Neil acted.

"Norma," he said, "if you really believe that your future lies in the copy department, I wouldn't stand in your way. But first you have to show me that you can really fit in, there. Things haven't always gone so well between you and them. We'd *all* be better off if you could work more smoothly with them—even as an account executive. Now, is it personal, or what?"

This didn't win Neil the whole ball game, but it gave him a start. He understood Norma's real motivation, and he had begun to use it in the direction he wanted it to go.

5. SEIZING THE KEY OF CAUSE AND EFFECT

People almost always give out signs that show how they really feel—if we can only understand. What they say, what they do and how they do it—these can tell us a great deal if we read them

correctly. Changes in a person's typical pattern of behavior
—talking and acting—indicate significant changes "inside" that
person, that we may need to understand if we are to deal with that
person effectively, in a planned way. The feelings that are strong
enough to affect someone's overt behavior are strong enough to be
quite motivating.

Many feelings are not "hooked up" yet: they come into exis-
tence and they churn around inside a person, and they may show,
but they do not immediately lead to intelligently motivated activities. Anger, hatred, fear, resentment—such emotions as these
cause unhappiness, and often lead to illogical, unthought-out behavior. Joy, delight, affection, confidence, enthusiasm—such emotions as these may also lead to "demonstrative behavior" that
serves no conscious, deliberate purpose. But such manifestations of
feeling offer us valuable clues as to the emotional make-up of the
persons involved, and so can help us to understand feelings that lend
power to motivations.

Taking Advantage of People's Moods and Emotions

Every intelligent employee instinctively waits for the boss to be
"in a good mood" before he asks for a raise. Every salesman
—well, almost every salesman—knows enough not to press for an
order when he finds a prospect disturbed, annoyed, upset. Even
very young children learn how to wait, in order to ask parents for
special privileges and favors when father or mother is cheerful and
pleased—not when they are "aggravated." These are elementary,
intuitive examples of the importance of an individual's emotional
state for the motivating of that individual by others. The individual's
emotion can oppose a motivation, or support it, or just distract him.
And the strength of the opposition or of the support or the degree of
distraction, will tend to be in proportion to the strength of the
emotion—and to the degree to which the emotion and the motivation are related.

When a vice president retired from a large trucking company,
three senior executives were candidates for his job. One of them got
it. The other two were both greatly disappointed, but they reacted
differently.

Melvin D. was terribly frustrated and upset when he heard the
bad news. He actually broke some things, and he even cried a little.

That night he got drunk. In the following days he became sour, frowned constantly, and grew increasingly difficult. His subordinates learned to recognize his intensifying new orientation: he tended to be negative about all ideas and suggestions; highly critical of everyone; and especially, bitterly critical of the successful candidate.

Recognizing and Handling Attitudes that Are Negative or Destructive

Some of those closest to Melvin D. came to realize that what had started as a strong but purposeless emotion, born of intense frustration, was being converted into a powerful motivation—one openly aimed at asserting his individuality; but also, increasingly though less obviously, at attacking and undercutting his successful rival. Sooner or later, some of those who sought to influence him learned that he could be greatly influenced by considerations of the expected effect upon his enemy: opposing a favorable effect, and favoring an adverse effect. And so Melvin D.'s spontaneous but intense disappointment was soon transformed into a systematic vendetta against the man who had beaten him. Frustration became hostility; and hostility motivated behavior that fed Melvin D.'s now perverse satisfactions.

Using Disappointments and Frustrations to Learn What You Need to Succeed

The other disappointed candidate, Solly F., was also frustrated. He didn't come into the office for several days; he sat at home, thinking things through. He was consciously readjusting his hopes, ambitions and expectations to the new reality. He saw that, somehow, he had *not* been *the* outstanding candidate in the eyes of the Board Of Directors.

So he studied his own strengths and weaknesses; and he tried to see himself as the Board members would see him. He tried to learn, from all this, how to become a more successful candidate for the next vice-presidential opening. He was still ambitious, perhaps more so than ever, to become a vice-president—despite (and perhaps all the more because of) his disappointment. He worked and tried harder than before; and his ambition motivated him to the constructive behavior that he believed and hoped would foster his promotion.

Thus two men who suffered disappointment and frustration over the same event underwent emotional reactions that motivated them in entirely different—really opposite—ways. It would not be enough to understand that Melvin D. and Solly F. had both been disappointed and frustrated. To understand their very different motivations it would be essential also to understand the resentment and bitterness that led to negativism and ego-compensatory behavior in one; and the persistent ambition and determination that kept the other trying harder than ever to be a more valuable and constructive and appreciated member of the management team.

It was not difficult to analyze and understand the motivations of these two if one had the opportunity to observe their behavior *after* their disappointment. But it would have been quite risky to *predict* beforehand what their motivations—and their behavior —would be. Perhaps some associates who knew them well could have done this fairly accurately, perhaps not. Some friends of both were surprised at their reactions—a few extremely so. In any case, to assume any particular motivation in advance would surely be rather chancy. Far better to infer it from the behavior that spelled it out.

As soon as Melvin D. and Solly F. began to behave in a manner consistent with their motivations, it was easy to see *why* they did so, even though they reacted differently to the same disappointment. Anyone who knew them both before could understand that they *were* reacting to the big disappointment; and that the great difference in their reactions was due to "how they took it"—and they took it differently because of individual differences in their characters, in their personalities, and in their personal lives and situations.

Understanding Reactions that Hinder Your Purpose, and Those that Help

A bright young newcomer to the same organization was commenting to a friendly old-timer about the surprising differences between Melvin D. and Solly F.

"Funny thing," the old-timer replied, "about why they are the way they are, now. Used to be, there wasn't all that much difference between them. They were both bucking for the big job, along with Mr. P. and Mr. P. got it. So they both changed—a lot. Melvin D.

got to be a terrible old sour-puss; and Solly F. turned into a real eager-beaver. Personally, I think Melvin D. got hurt in the ego, and Solly F. only got hurt in the hope department. So now Melvin D. lets his nasty old ego show, he doesn't care how; he's trying to prove something to himself. But Solly F. just tries harder than ever; he wants to prove something to the Directors, and maybe to himself. That's how they are; and you'll be able to understand them better, now that you know why."

Experience is the teacher; people learn from experience— whatever they do learn; and whether they want to or not. Melvin D. learned to solace his wounded ego by indulging himself in negativism and criticism and sniping; Solly F. learned to try to justify his ego by proving his real worth. From the same event each had a very different *personal* experience. Understanding of the individual experience that lay behind each individual's behavior would be essential to understanding their motivations—*why* each one behaved as he did. Understanding their characters would be made easier by understanding the *experience* that affected the motivations of each.

Anyone who wanted to motivate Melvin D. or Solly F. now would need to understand their very different kinds of motivation or reaction to motivation. Just knowing their usual pattern of behavior might not be enough. To motivate them most surely and effectively, a person would need to have some understanding of *WHY* they behave the way they do. That way, each could be motivated on a basis that really fits *him*.

Perhaps there was a wise old boy on the Board of Directors, who had said: "Melvin D. and Solly F. are both good men; and both are young enough to wait. Let's give it to P., and then we'll see how Melvin D. and Solly F. take it. We'll find out if they discourage easily. And we'll find out if they try harder than ever, after a disappointment. That way we'll know more about their motivations, and that will help when the next vacancy comes up."

5

HOW TO SET UP
A PROGRAM FOR
MOTIVATIONAL LEVERAGE

To apply Motivational Leverage, not only successfully but also in the easiest and most effective way, you will need a *plan*—a sound, intelligent plan that makes the most of whatever you have going for you. This chapter tells you how to go about making a *target plan* that will be most likely to produce the results you are after.

1. TARGETING FOR YOUR OBJECTIVES

Roscoe L. was one of eight junior purchasing agents in the Chicago head office of a large manufacturing company. He wanted the appointment as chief purchasing agent for a new plant to be opened by the company in Massachussetts. That appointment was his *target*. (See Figure 1a.) He was really motivated to reach that *target*.

In order to receive this appointment, he would have to be picked for it by his boss, Lester D., the senior purchasing agent.

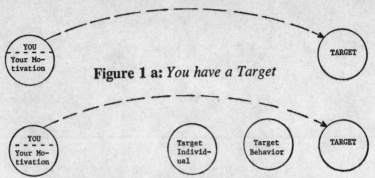

Figure 1 a: *You have a Target*

Figure 1 b: *You identify the individual who can make it possible for you to get what you want*

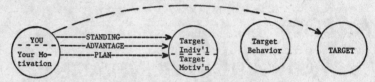

Figure 1 c: *You identify the motivations you can use; evaluate your Standing; consider possible Advantages; and make your Plan for developing the Leverage you will need*

Figure 1 d: *You adjust your own Behavior to maximize your Standing and increase your Advantage in accordance with your Plan to develop the Leverage you need*

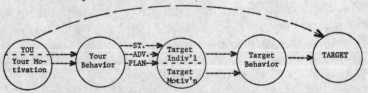

Figure 1 e: *Bingo! As you succeed in carrying out your Plan by applying the Motivational Leverage you have developed, the Target Individual will be motivated to behavior that will bring you to your Target*

That made Lester D. the *target individual*. (See Figure 1b.) Only action by the *target individual* could bring Roscoe L. to his *target*.

Roscoe had a certain *standing* with Lester (see Figure 1c), just as one of his subordinates, but so did all the other seven junior purchasing agents under Lester in the same office. What made or could make his *standing* different than theirs? Better than theirs? More likely than theirs to help motivate the senior agent as Roscoe wanted to motivate him?

How Roscoe L. Used His *Advantages* to Improve His *Standing*

Roscoe figured that he had some *advantages* that he could use. (See Figure 1c.) He realized that some of his competitors for the job also had *advantages*, and perhaps more or better *advantages* than he. But he figured both on adding to his *advantages* and on using them advantageously, for maximum *leverage* to motivate Lester.

Then Roscoe began thinking seriously about Lester's motivations. He decided that, in all probability, Lester would have as a basic motivation the placing of a man in the new post who would handle the job most competently, and also cause the least trouble requiring intervention or assistance from the head office. But Lester would not like to lose anyone he *needed*: he would greatly prefer to give up from his staff the candidate who would be most easily replaced—whose loss would be least felt. Would this be a contradiction?

Roscoe thought a lot about Lester, and about these probable motivations. He checked them out as well as he could, by studying how Lester had made a few similar selections in the past; by considering Lester's general character and disposition and patterns of behavior; and by evaluating the shreds of wisdom among the chaff in the inevitable discussions that took place in the office about who wanted and who would get the upcoming job in Massachusetts.

Roscoe finally decided he was right about Lester's motivations—the motivations of the *target individual*–the *target motivations*—the motivations he would have to act upon if he were to reach his *target*. Lester would want to pick the best man for the job, providing he could be spared from, or replaced in, Lester's own operation.

Having decided this, Roscoe made his *target plan*. (See Figure 1c.)

Making a *Target Plan*

Roscoe studied the company objectives for the new plant. He made himself familiar with the kinds of equipment and supplies and materials that would have to be purchased. He managed to let Lester know that he was doing this. It helped his *standing,* and it gave him some additional *advantage*. (See Figure 1c.)

Roscoe knew that he would need at least one powerful *advantage,* to use as *leverage* to "move" Lester. What could Roscoe use as an *advantage*? Among the items Roscoe was already buying regularly were a number of the items that would have to be bought for the new plant. Roscoe made a list of these, and put in some time figuring out the best sources of supply for delivery to Massachusetts. He was able to work out a few advantageous possibilities.

He showed all this to Lester, and asked Lester's permission to make similar studies for other items—not regularly purchased by him. After some thought, Lester O.K.'d a few studies on some critical items where geographical factors might make a substantial difference. Roscoe made it a point to come up with some pretty good answers, but especially to demonstrate his ability to solve non-routine problems in a responsible way. Lester was impressed; Roscoe's *standing* improved. And his *advantages* increased substantially.

One day Roscoe felt his *target plan* was far enough along, and the deadline for Lester to make his decision was close enough, for the timing to be right for him to work directly, face-to-face, on the *target motivations*. He asked Lester for a conference, and suggested lunch.

With the coffee, Roscoe summarized the fact that he wanted the appointment to Massachusetts, and had done all he could to qualify himself in advance for it. He emphasized the factors that gave him *standing,* and he dwelt heavily upon his *advantages*. And when he had given all these the full treatment, he pulled out the clincher.

How to Create a Big *Advantage*

"I know you will be thinking about the replacement of anyone you decide to send to Massachusetts. Naturally. And, of course, I realize that I am practically indispensable! Well, I'm going to tell you a secret I wouldn't tell anybody else—especially not my wife! I'm going to tell you how to get along without me!

"First of all, about one third of the most active items I handle now, I will also be buying for Massachusetts. These purchases can be combined, with separate deliveries, so I can take care of that for you, even when I am there. Second, on my vacations and when I have been sick, Lem S. has been handling my work. He knows the principal items and the leading sources. That can help the transition. Finally, I wouldn't be leaving for Massachusetts for at least three months. You can hire my replacement any time, now, and I'll have at least a month or two to break him in. I already have my job description up to date, with complete lists of items, with sources of supply, with contact names, recent price ranges—all organized and ready to turn over. How's that for laying my head on the block? All you have to do is chop it off—and send it to Massachusetts!''

How It Helps You to Understand the Situation as a Whole

Roscoe's *motivation,* working through his *behavior,* was adding to his *advantages* working on the *target motivation.* His *target plan* was working on the *motivation target.* And when Lester asked himself *"Why not* pick Roscoe for the Massachusetts job?'' he found he could justify the choice, because Roscoe's *standing* was such as to make it seem logical, reasonable and right. *(See Figure 1d.)* Roscoe's Motivational Leverage was really working.

The *target motivation* worked upon the *target behavior:* Lester made his decision—and Roscoe reached his *target.* (See Figure 1e.)

The process illustrated by this example is basic, and it has been presented in this diagrammatic form (Figures 1a-e) to make it as easy as possible to understand the fundamental relationships involved.

To motivate another person effectively, it *is* necessary to understand the situation as a *whole.* The integral, inseparable elements or steps are listed below.

Making a Good *Target Plan*, and Making It Work

1. Identify *your* goal, objective, purpose, etc.—your *target*—as clearly and specifically as possible.
2. Identify the individual or individuals, the group, the body,

etc.—the *target individual(s)*—that must be motivated if you are to reach your *target*.

3. Consider your *standing* with the *target individual*.
4. Consider what *advantage(s)* you have that may be used in motivating the *target individual*. Consider also what *advantage(s)* you can create.
5. Consider what are the motivations of the *target individual*; and which of these you can use as *target motivation(s)*.
6. Develop your *target plan*, using your *standing* and your *advantages* for Motivational Leverage on the *target motivation(s)*.
7. Operate your *target plan*, strengthening and adding to your *standing* and building your *advantages(s)*, always focussed on the *target motivation(s)*.
8. Observe carefully all *target individual* reactions and significant changes of behavior; and adjust your *behavior* accordingly. Follow up success; and drop *behavior* that appears ineffective for your purposes.
9. Keep up your Motivational Leverage until you reach the *target*.

2. HOW TO TIME YOUR TARGET PLAN FOR GREATEST EFFECT

The wisdom of past generations is often distilled into bits of proverbial advice; and some of these seem to contradict one another. For instance, "Strike while the iron is hot" urges immediate action; while "He who fights and runs away will live to fight another day" suggests that a final settlement can always be put off.

However, the wisdom in these proverbs is not so superficial. They both suggest the importance of timing, and give some hints about this. *When* is the iron hot enough? And *when* is "another day"? If you do not strike while the iron is hot (an obvious reference to the blacksmith pounding the white-hot iron into shape on his anvil) you will have to heat the iron up again. This is something like running away "to fight another day." The one expression emphasizes avoidance of delay; the other appears to suggest postponement. Both are concerned with *timing*—acting at the *most* advantageous moment, and *not* acting at a disadvantageous moment.

Timing can be a major factor—indeed, the decisive one—in

the motivation of a *target individual* for a specific purpose. The right moment can make all the difference. It is often very important to coordinate your *target plan* with more or less related events. It is also true that occasions sometimes arise, unexpectedly, which offer you very favorable opportunities for motivating a *target individual*—*if* you are ready, and *if* you know how to seize the moment. And then there is the wrong time, when an adverse motivation would more probably occur, and such occasions should, if possible, be avoided. Let us illustrate these three problems of timing.

How to Plan When You Have Plenty of Time

Oscar P. was one of six Assistant Buyers in the very large furniture department of a very large retail operation. His boss, the Senior Buyer, was sixty-two years old and would have to retire in three years. All six of the Assistant Buyers would be candidates to succeed him, but the final decision would not be made for more than two years, even though there would be progress made toward a decision as the qualifications of the leading contenders were evaluated. Ultimately, the Senior Buyer would make his recommendation (which would almost certainly be accepted by top management) in time for the successful candidate to be trained and prepared for his new responsibilities before the Senior Buyer's scheduled retirement.

Oscar was determined to be the one chosen. To succeed in this, he knew he would have to motivate the Senior Buyer to choose him. So he worked out a carefully timed *target plan*, with the Senior Buyer as the *target individual*. He had *standing* as an Assistant Buyer, but only as one of the six competitors for the target position. He had *advantages* in being able to and in having opportunity to demonstrate what he could do—but the other five competitors had similar *advantages*. It was up to him to develop his *advantages* into better Motivational Leverage than the others'; and to improve his *standing* so that, when the time came, he would be the one chosen.

Oscar went over his own regular activities, and compared them with the responsibilities of the Senior Buyer. He concluded that the *target individual* would be motivated to make his decision on the basis of such abilities as negotiation with vendors, budgeting, sales forecasting, planning, pricing, merchandising, handling and training of junior buyers and other personnel, and general administrative duties. He then picked specific opportunities—certain scheduled situations—when he would have special opportunities to demonstrate his qualifications in these critical areas. He planned to use these opportunities systematically to develop his *advantages* in relation to the *target motivation*.

He had more than two years in which to carry out his *target plan;* and this gave him a number of occasions for demonstrating his capabilities in relation to the *target factors*—the factors on the basis of which the Motivational Leverage would operate.

His five competitors had similar, parallel *advantages* and opportunities, and were similarly motivated to show what they could do. But they did not develop systematic *target plans,* like Oscar. And so they did not *time* their activities for effectiveness in developing their *advantages,* the way Oscar did. As a result, Oscar built his *standing* with the Senior Buyer steadily, systematically, on every occasion, with every opportunity he could foresee. According to schedule, Oscar's *standing* rose cumulatively, and when the time came, the Senior Buyer gave him the nod—all according to Oscar's *motivation plan.* Timing was a major element in Oscar's successful application of Motivational Leverage.

How to Be Ready for the Right Moment

There is another kind of timing which involves seizing "the right instant"—"the psychological moment"—the precise point in time when the *target individual* is most receptive, and the *target motivation* is strongest. Sometimes the motivator's *standing* is momentarily or suddenly high; sometimes his *advantages* stand out, and his *leverage* is at a peak. If he can capitalize on such developments, he can succeed in his *target plan* almost instantaneously.

Lem T. was an excellent salesman; but he was also a fun-loving bachelor. He had a certain reputation for irresponsibility and for dubious behavior when on the road. At the same time, he had good relations with his customers, knew the product line and its applications thoroughly, and was intelligent and capable. Lem's company had to fill a vacancy for Sales Manager of the Western District, and Lem had indicated his interest in the position; but the General Sales Manager refused to take him seriously when he asked to be considered.

But Lem had a secret *advantage* he knew would greatly improve his *standing* and give him the *leverage* he needed. He made his *target plan* and put it into effect quickly.

A few days later, Lem announced his engagement to be married! The incorrigible bachelor was going to take a wife! It was the talk of the office. The General Sales Manager called him in, congratulated him, and wished him luck. With perfect timing, Lem "struck while the iron was hot."

"I know you have been thinking of me as a pretty wild guy," Lem said. "Well, that's all over, now. I'm settling down. And I mean just that. I've been luckier than I deserve—I've found the girl who can make me toe the line and like it—and now I'm out to get ahead in the world so my family can be proud of me. *And I want that job!* You make me Manager of that Western District and you'll be glad you did. I'm out to show you what I can do. I know you were worried about my personal conduct, but that's all over now. You couldn't have anything else against me. You know I know the line, and I know all the applications; and you know I get along fine with customers and with the other men; and you know I can sell! So, look at me like I *am–now*! Make *me* Manager of the Western District! You'll never by sorry!"

Lem got the job. What he had done was to change his *standing*–almost overnight. He had overcome the single deficiency in his *standing*—and that enabled him to use his *advantages* effectively. And so, like a good salesman, he had seized the opportunity. His timing was perfect, and it got him the promotion and higher pay that he was after.

Knowing When It Is Best to Postpone

The other kind of timing involves postponement—but constructive postponement.

Luke A. was going through his annual evaluation interview with his supervisor. Luke wanted a raise, and had planned to ask for it during this review. But he saw that his supervisor was quite critical of Luke's behavior toward some of the juniors in the department—one girl had been so upset when Luke criticized her work that she had quit.

Luke quickly realized that he could have a much better *standing* if he let a little time pass, and if he used this time to show his supervisor that the unfortunate episode with the girl was exceptional—that he really had good relations with the juniors.

This tactical postponement saved Luke from being turned down, and gave him the chance to build up his *standing* until he could expect to motivate his *target individual* successfully, which he later did.

These three examples illustrate the great importance of timing when putting your *target plan* into effect; and in making the *target plan* fit the timing.

3. HOW TO MAKE YOUR *TARGET PLAN* FIT THE REAL SITUATION

Your *target plan* must fit the actual situation if it is to work out as you wish. To make it fit, it is often necessary to explore the situation. There may be important elements or factors in the situation that you do not know enough about, so you had better explore, or your *plan* may be way off from what you need.

Lew N., president of Columbia Castings Company, had been concerned about the performance of his Vice President for Marketing, Ted S., who seemed to have lost a lot of his earlier energy, interest and zest. Where he had formerly travelled vigorously to work with the field sales organization, he now stayed in the home office. Where he had often worked late, he now regularly left at five o'clock or earlier. Where before he had clearly shown his zealous concern, he now seemed to have lost interest.

Lew had called Ted into a conference, and had frankly asked him what was holding him back. Ted had indignantly denied any such condition. Lew, having in mind Ted's long-displayed value to the company, and wishing to motivate him to renewed efforts, called him in again, a week later. This time he offered an incentive —an attractive stock option for more effective performance. But Ted did not seem very appreciative of this offer.

As Lew became more and more concerned about Ted, he kept asking the Marketing Department for information; and he occasionally called up some of the District Sales Managers to check on the situation. He requested some special reports; and whenever he saw Ted he would ask, quite meaningfully, how things were going. After about three months of this, Ted coldly handed in his resignation. In a few weeks he was at work for another company, in a different industry. And Lew learned that he was not being paid any more than before.

What had happened?

Exploring the Situation to Understand It Better

Ted S. was rather proud and sensitive, conscious of his own abilities, and capable of much hard work and enthusiasm. But he needed praise and appreciation to keep him motivated to function at the top of his form. Lew had failed to give Ted the necessary encouragement. And then, when Ted slowed down for lack of appreciation, praise and special reward for his good work, Lew had called him in and, in effect, criticized him for lying down on the job (at least, that's the way it seemed to Ted). When Lew began to make inquiries and ask leading questions, Ted felt that he was being checked up on—even spied upon—and that Lew was also nagging him. Under these conditions he viewed the offer of a stock option more as a reproof than a reward: in effect, Lew was offering him an incentive for doing what he felt he had already been doing without such an incentive; and—Ted believed—Lew did this without realizing or acknowledging the real extent of Ted's efforts and the value of his contribution.

Lew had failed to explore the situation properly, or he would have realized that Ted had needed and wanted recognition and reward *before*, when he had been performing extremely well. Failure to explore caused Lew to ignore the need to motivate Ted when suitable motivation was needed. But because he had failed to explore properly, Lew also acted inappropriately, after he saw the need to motivate Ted. And, finally, Lew's behavior in trying to explore the effects of his attempt to motivate Ted was inappropriate, and only succeeded in further alienating Ted, who thought of it as spying, and who had then decided to look for a position where he would be appreciated, and so be happier.

Advantages of Exploring the Situation

Lew should have been aware that Ted needed encouragement and praise and appreciation; that he needed to feel that he was a truly valuable member of the top-management team. And only Lew was in a position to give him that kind of "reward" on a properly authoritative basis.

It wouldn't have taken a great deal of "exploration" for Lew to have gained a very adequate understanding of this. Such needs and wants, such dependence on encouragement are extremely common; and the signs are easy to read. Ted often spoke of his exploits in ways that clearly invited approval; and his reaction to approval —when given—was clearly one of great satisfaction. Once Lew could see Ted as a *target individual* he could readily have spotted approbation as a *target motivation* of major importance. He would then have realized his own very special *standing,* as president, for according approbation; and his great *advantage,* also as president, in being in a position to judge Ted's performance and merits.

But Lew's failure to explore in the first place had an anti- (or negatively) motivating result. Because of Lew's *standing,* his failure to satisfy Ted's need for approbation had a serious effect, which was resented. Similarly, when Lew did try to explore the developing situation in an effort to determine if his attempt to motivate Ted was working, Lew's *standing*—as the only person who *could* check up on Ted, and the only person in a position to criticize him or even to imply criticism—made the appearance of spying and nagging especially unacceptable, and aggravated Ted's resentment.

What to Avoid When You Explore

This case illustrates both the need for adequate exploration, if an individual is to be successfully motivated, and the danger of having exploration attempts interfere with the process of motivation.

People who may accept motivation and who react to it as planned will, nevertheless, resent any feeling of being *manipulated.* The feeling that "*I* am getting what *I* want out of this" is generally sufficient to balance the recognition that "*you* are getting what *you* want," when a *motivation plan* is successfully carried out. But if an individual (or a group) gets the impression that someone (or some group, such as "management") is knowingly and skillfully operating to change his (or their) behavior, he (or they) may resent it. No one wants to feel like a puppet, controlled by a master-puppeteer, pulling strings. When the *target individual* (or *target group*) gets a feeling like that, the result can be extremely counter-productive; they may become motivated to do something like the exact opposite of what the *target plan* calls for.

How to Make Your Exploring Help Your *Standing*

The differences between exploratory behavior that contributes to successful motivation and exploratory behavior that arouses resentment and opposition may be slight—even subtle and difficult to identify. But it is nonetheless real, important, and necessary to understand, if the undesirable consequences are to be avoided.

Essentially, we are dealing here again with the Self-Image —the Image of the Self discussed in Chapter 4. People rarely resent inquiry into their goals and interests, their aspirations and hopes —even their needs and wants—when the inquiry comes from someone they believe to have a sincere, altruistic, empathic or even sympathetic attitude toward them. In fact, they are usually pleased, gratified, even flattered when such interest is displayed, especially if this is from someone they like or admire, or someone above them in an organizational structure. This kind of exploring can really help your *standing* with them.

But all this depends on the interest being shown in such a way as to maintain and support the *self-concept* of the individual. The exploration must be, essentially, *respectful*. It must contribute to and not detract from the dignity of the individual. The interest shown must be contructive: it must show due recognition of the individual's worth, and of the values that move him. Once there is an apprearance of coldness, of manipulation, of special, hidden motivation, then uneasiness and resentment take the place of gratification. If the tone of the exploration is the least bit patronizing or manipulative, great harm may be done.

The real test is in the basic attitude felt by the *motivator* toward the *motivatee*. If this attitude is not helpful to or in the interest of the *motivatee*, there is a reasonably strong likelihood that he will sense it, and become defensive. After all, exploration is not a one-way street!

But there is no substitute for exploration of the situation when it comes to setting up a *target plan* that will get you to your *target*, through *leverage*, toward the necessary *target behavior* by the *target individual*.

4. HOW TO TEST YOUR PLAN TO MAKE SURE IT CAN WORK

Before you decide on any of the primary components for a

target plan, it is a good idea to test the ideas you are considering. Otherwise, of course, you may develop a *target plan* based on false impressions, beliefs or ideas. If you spend your time and effort trying to put such a plan into effect, you would at best be working on a plan less well-adapted to your purpose than might otherwise be the case; and at worst it could bring about poor results, or even the wrong results.

Asking Yourself the Right Questions

Begin your testing by asking yourself questions like these:

Who is the best target individual? If there are several individuals who are in a position to help you to the *target,* you will want to choose the one who is most influential. But you may not find a *target motivation* in that one, that you can manage to use; or your *standing* may be inadequate; or you may not have a strong enough *advantage.* You may have a better chance with someone who may be somewhat less influential for your *target purpose,* but who has a *target motivation* you can work on effectively; or with whom your *standing* or your *advantages* are particularly likely to give you better Motivational Leverage.

How to Use *Chain Motivation*

Of course, this second person, if strongly enough motivated, may act to motivate the person you cannot motivate directly. This is called *chain motivation,* and it is especially applicable in organizations, or in other relationships involving numbers of people. You have seen this as a common tactic in families, where children often motivate the mother to motivate the father, or vice versa, for their own particular *target purposes.* And, of course, there is no special reason why you cannot work toward motivating more than one *target individual* at a time, if this will help to bring you to your *target.*

But in selecting a *target individual* it is especially necessary to be certain that the individual selected is actually likely to show, or is capable of the *target behavior* that you desire; and if he is, that he is likely to act as you wish because of the *leverage* that you, with your *standing,* and your available *advantages,* can bring to bear on his *target motivation.*

Alfred M. was Assistant Controller of the Boyden Tool Company. Now he wanted to be transferred to the Manufacturing Department, as manager of the Accounting and Costs Section, since that post became suddenly vacant. He decided that the best route to go was to motivate his boss, the Controller, to speak for him to the Vice President-Manufacturing. That was a planned *chain motivation*—Alfred to motivate the Controller to motivate the Vice President to the *target behavior* that would bring Alfred to his *target*.

Alfred spent some time figuring out what *target motivation* to use on the Controller. Alfred himself was due for a promotion, and a favorite subordinate of the Controller, fully qualified, could be promoted to Alfred's place; but the Controller himself had no place to go and was years from retirement. Alfred's *standing* was excellent, and he had several *advantages:* he was well qualified for the post he wanted; the post was vacant and had to be filled; there was no other obvious candidate; and—of course—Alfred could always resign if he felt his path upward was blocked.

He wove all these into a very convincing argument, exploiting his *standing* and his *advantages* very skillfully against every one of the Contoller's known *target motivations*. But, in the end, he learned that he was wasting his time. He ran into a roadblock he didn't know was there. Finally the Controller told him what it was.

Making Sure You Have the Right *Target Individual*

"Alfred, everything you say is true. And I'd really like to help you. You *are* well qualified for that position. You *do* deserve to have the promotion. You *have* trained your replacement. You'd do a good job there, and the company would benefit. All that is true. I admit it. I agree. And furthermore, I'd really like to see you get that job, and you have my permission and approval to go after it. But—Alfred—you'll have to excuse me—I'm not going to Mr. B. (the Vice President-Manufacturing) for you. Don't ask me why. I'm truly sorry not to do this for you; but I can't."

It was a long time before Alfred found out the reason: it was personal and "political." Those two men were not on friendly terms; they had had a serious dispute about a budget matter a year previously, and there had been another disagreement in the Executive Committee only a few days before. The Controller honestly felt that he simply couldn't go to the other man and ask consideration for his own assistant.

Alfred thus found that the Controller was not a suitable *target individual:* there was a special reason why it would be extremely difficult—almost impossible—to motivate him to the desired *target behavior,* and then he might not be effective in the desired way.

Such special conditions often exist; and if exploration does not uncover them, then appropriate testing may. (Fortunately Alfred M., with nothing to lose, made the Vice President-Manufacturing his *target individual,* went to him directly, and got the position he wanted.)

Once you have made certain—as far as you can—that your choice of *target individual* is well founded, and have identified one or more *target motivations,* ask yourself a few more questions.

How to Check Out *Target Moitvations*

Is (are) this (these) target motivation(s) potentially strong enough? The best way to check or test this is to determine whether, in the past, the *target individual* has been moved to behavior similar to the desired TARGET *behavior* by motivation(s) similar to the *target motivation.* If something like this has happened before, and you can uncover no reason why it should not happen again (conditions do change, and this can affect changes in patterns of behavior) then you are probably justified in expecting it to occur again. But if there is no such favorable precedent, you had better check very carefully your assumptions about the *target motivation.*

Is your standing with the' target individual such as to make realistic your hope of his target behavior on your behalf? Even people who love you, who like and admire you, will not do everything you ask them to do.

The ethical Dean of Admissions will not admit his own son to the college if he knows him to be unqualified. The honest banker will not make a loan to his own brother, if the credit standing is inadequate, etc.

Predicting *Target Behavior*

And then again, there is always a certain proportion (however indeterminable) between *standing* and *target behavior.* The corporation president may go to lunch with a competitor, but perhaps not with one of his own junior subordinates. Those in a position to decide promotions are often influenced by personal factors. Those in a position to decide which supplier gets an order are often moved by factors other than price, quality, value, delivery, etc. *Standing* should generally be regarded as a *limiting* factor: if adequate, it does not assure *target behavior*; but if inadequate, it renders the desired *target behavior* unlikely.

No one ever really knows what his *standing* is with anyone else—especially with a *target individual*. And it can change from moment to moment—even from mood to mood! But it is most desirable to think as clearly and objectively as possible about one's *standing*. It may be necessary to work to change it, to improve it, so that your *advantage(s)* can give the Motivational Leverage you need toward the *target motivation*.

How to Test Your *Standing* and *Advantages*

Is (are) your advantage(s) strong enough to bring about target behavior? As with *standing,* this should be carefully and objectively weighed. Perhaps your *advantage* needs to be increased; or perhaps you need other *advantages* to reinforce it.

Sometimes *standing* and/or *advantage* can actually be tested by applying them to test situations, like asking for lesser *target behavior* and carefully evaluating the results. Much can be learned in this way; but care should be taken not to allow the testing to alter the conditions. Ill-conceived testing can lower *standing* and reduce *advantages*.

But some degree of testing is usually possible; and it should be applied to the important elements of the *target plan* in order to be as sure as possible that the plan does fit the actual conditions, and can be reasonably expected to produce the *target behavior* that you are after.

5. HOW TO PUT IT ALL TOGETHER SO YOUR PLAN COMES OUT RIGHT

Steve F. is Regional Service Manager for the West Coast of the Bloor Machinery Company. His district manager for Southern California has just quit, to join a competitor. Steve needs to put in a very competent man, as a replacement, as soon as possible. That is his need. His problem—how to meet this need—involves, first, picking a good man from those available, and then motivating that man to take the job.

He looks over the service engineers that perform in his region, and he comes to the conclusion that one man—Ralph G.—is by far the best one for the job. Ralph has part of the Bay Area—in San Francisco—as his territory. He has done a beautiful job there, and Steve knows that Ralph can service their customers down south as well as the man who quit, if anyone can.

So now he has come to a decision about the first part of his problem—WHO? But that decision is worthless, and the problem has to be solved differently, if Ralph G. doesn't want to move from San Francisco to Los Angeles. How to motivate him?

Steve knows that Ralph has just moved into a new house near Palo Alto. It is the fall of the year; Ralph's children have already started school. Ralph's wife is a Bay Area girl; her family and friends are all around there, and she will not want to move away. But Steve knows that, somehow, he will have to find a way to persuade Ralph to take over that L.A. territory. What can he do to motivate him? What *target plan* can succeed?

Thinking about the Needs of the Target Individual

Steve begins thinking about Ralph's *needs*—the needs he is now satisfying, and will not want to give up on; and the needs he has that may not be satisfied now. And Steve thinks in terms of what *he* can do to take away as little as possible of what Ralph has and wants to keep, while doing what he can to add something that will make Ralph want to—or at least willing to—make the change. To motivate Ralph, Steve knows he must both *meet objections*, and *offer inducements*.

Of course, if Steve could offer a large enough financial inducement, this alone might overcome Ralph's objections. But Steve does not have the power or the authority to go beyond the regular compensation structure of the company; and the company has rather strict policies controlling compensation. So Steve knows he can go only so far in this direction. And this alone will not be enough to overcome Ralph's objections. So he will have to think about what else he can do. Steve has to "add things up and come out right."

Picking the Moment and Setting the Stage

When he has finally worked out his plan, Steve arranges to

spend a day and evening with Ralph, and so he flies to San Francisco. Ralph picks him up at the airport motel early the next morning. They have breakfast together, and Steve goes along with Ralph on his calls all day (as they are accustomed to doing every few months).

After the last call, Steve has Ralph drive to a good restaurant, and they settle down for a well-nourished evening. It is now or never for Steve's plan.

"Ralph," he begins, "I always look forward to putting in a day with you. It's a pleasure to see the way you have built such good relations with our customers; and I always learn something, too—like today—how to adjust that speed control on the KF-78. I'm going to put that in the Service Bulletin. That's really a good point.

"Now, let's talk about you. Some people think you're a little young to be a District Service Manager; but as far as I'm concerned, you're in line for the next spot that opens up. And there's one opening up right now. You know about it—it's in L.A."

How Steve F. Showed that He Had Been Thinking About Needs

"Well, Ralph, as soon as I thought about you for that opening, I realized that I'd be asking you to make something of a sacrifice. I know about your new house, and the kids in school, and Maud's family, and all that. And I want you to know that I've really been thinking about how to make things easy for you to accept this opportunity.

"So here's what I came up with. You can handle that district, and do it without moving your family! You can get down there Monday mornings and you can get back Fridays. In fact, you can arrange matters so you take care of the paperwork up here, one or two days a week, and only go down there to handle the supervision of the men and the necessary customer contacts.

"I'll fix you up with an expense account that will take care of your extra travel and anything else that's reasonable. I know you'll give the job all you can, so if you're not down there every day I won't worry about it. And I'll explain it to the men you'll have reporting to you—we'll have a meeting when I install you down there.

"Now, about the future. I'll leave it up to you. If you do decide

to move down to L.A. after the school year, the company will help
you to move, as we always do, and help you sell or rent your house
here—that shouldn't be a problem. I know Maud prefers to be in
this area, but you can explain to her that we just don't have a district
manager job open here, now; I'm sure you'll agree that Art G. is
doing a good job for us. But if Art leaves, or if we move him, I
promise to give you a crack at the job here in Frisco, if you want to
transfer back up here.

"Now, Ralph, you know the score. If you want to get ahead in
any company that isn't just local, you have to be willing to move.
Naturally, some places are more pleasant or convenient than others.
But you have to look at the whole picture. If it's really more important to you to stay and live and work here than to move up, why—by
all means tell us so, and of course you can go on just as you have
been. You're doing a good job for us, of course—that's why I'm
offering you this chance. But if it's important to you to move up,
well—I'll make it just as easy for you as I can."

How Putting It All Together Can Really Do the Job for You

Steve had really added it all up. Ralph didn't even need to state
his objections—Steve had already anticipated them, and had offered
to do everything within reason to meet them. The promotion would
be a big plus—Ralph really didn't have the heart to turn it down,
since there was no telling when he'd get another chance. Ralph's
desire to move up, of course, was the *target motivation* that Steve
aimed at. And when Steve held out the hope of moving back to San
Francisco, well, then Ralph knew he had a clincher for his wife.

The promotion, of course, was the big motivator. But when
Steve thought through Ralph's objections in advance, and came up
with accommodations that eased them considerably and demonstrated his desire to be helpful, he made things as easy as possible
for Ralph to say "yes."

Steve was experienced and competent when it came to motivating his men. That's why he was regional manager. He made his own
analysis of the situation, based upon his knowledge of the facts. He
made up his mind as to which considerations were relevant, and
which were not. He developed answers to likely objections in advance; he was able to state Ralph's objections for him, and to
answer them, before Ralph could get all involved in pressing them

himself. He was able to motivate the man he wanted, to do what he wanted him to do. Steve added it all up for Ralph.

There was another advantage to Steve's handling of this situation. He knew that Ralph would have to motivate his wife, Maud, to accept the idea. The way he added it all up for Ralph made it easier for Ralph to present the situation to Maud. That was *chain motivation*.

Often, the person you are trying to motivate will resist because he feels he will not be able to convince someone else. Steve understood this, and provided for it. He covered the problems of school and of moving; and he even threw in the prospect of moving back to San Francisco.

No *one* of the satisfiers that Steve offered Ralph would have been enough, by itself. The promotion alone, however desirable, would not have been enough to motivate Ralph if his serious objections had not been met. These were extremely relevant, and Steve recognized this. He added it all up—and that *was* enough.

Having the right inducement, being willing and able to satisfy needs—these are essential for successful motivation. But "putting them all together" is also essential, unless a single motivator is strong enough—and then, really, there is no problem. If the simple offer of a promotion had been enough to induce Ralph to overcome all his objections himself, Steve would not have needed to anticipate and plan as he did. But it would not have been enough, and Steve knew it. So he added it all up.

6

ACHIEVING
MOTIVATIONAL LEVERAGE
WITH YOUR TARGET PLAN

If your *target plan* is to be well-founded and the Motivational Leverage you will develop is to be properly designed and wisely directed, then you should first put yourself in a position to be sure about the more important factors in the situations.

This chapter can help you to learn what you need to know, and to discover the importance and/or the truth of much of what you run into in the way of information, assumption, impression or insight.

1. HOW TO LISTEN FOR WHAT YOU NEED TO KNOW

If you really want to get along well with people, and especially if you want to motivate them, you *must* "make it a two-way street"—you *must* listen to them. There is nothing more annoying than a person who never listens to anyone else. There is no surer way to tell another person how little you think of him, than to pay no attention to what he says. There is something truly insulting about showing someone else that you have no interest in what they are saying, or even in what they may say. To motivate people, obviously, you have to get them to listen to you; and they are pretty unlikely to be willing to listen to you if they ever get the idea that you are not interested in listening to them.

And yet, some people reveal this lack of interest in what the other fellow has to say, all the time—or particularly at the wrong time. The only way this mistake can motivate people is the wrong way—the negative way—the opposite of the way they want to motivate them. When someone really turns people off, they are not likely to go out of their way to help him, to give him what he wants, or to do as he wishes them to do. On the contrary, they may react in so negative a way as to make a real effort to block him, to turn others against him, to keep him from getting what he wants.

Arthur G., a salesman, was trying to sell some new electrical equipment to the manager of a rather old factory. He told his story, made his points about the "benefits" of his equipment, and put a number of illustrated brochures on the manager's desk.

The manager picked up a brochure, glanced at it, and said:

"I see your equipment is painted black—" but he got no further. Arthur came right back at him.

"Yes, sir! We can deliver in any color, of course; but we made a study, and on the basis of that study we *know* that the best color for equipment like ours is black. We use the finest lacquer—" and so on, for five minutes.

When Arthur stopped a moment for breath, the manager tried to get a word in edgewise: "About delivery arrangements—" but Arthur picked that up and yakked away about equipment in stock, and immediate delivery by truck, and expert crating and handling, and so on.

Why the Manager Interrupted the Salesman

Finally the manager stood up, and interrupted Arthur.

"I don't believe I'm interested," he said.

Arthur was taken aback. "But—but" he tried to get his monologue going again, but the manager had had enough. That was it.

Now, the fact of the matter was that the company was planning to move its operation to an entirely new plant at a distant location. Planning was well along, and they could have used a lot of the equipment Arthur was selling. But the manager wanted to clarify a few points before entering into any negotiations for purchase.

First, he knew that the modern plant they were setting up was to have a carefully planned color scheme. The walls were to be a light green, and all equipment was to be an olive green. Arthur could have sold his equipment in olive green, but he never let himself hear about this. Second, the new plant had a railroad siding, and was far away from the factory that made Arthur's equipment. So the manager wanted to ask about rail shipment. But Arthur never let himself learn that, either.

As the manager sat there and listened to Arthur, he realized that Arthur wasn't paying any attention *to him*. Emotionally, he was offended, irritated, resentful. And, naturally, he didn't want to put up with any more of that annoyance—or with Arthur. But also, he realized that if he did go ahead with Arthur, the negotiations and arrangements would be all that much more difficult and time consuming, as well as unpleasant; and that there would be an added risk that significant points would be disregarded or passed over, as Arthur concentrated on his own thoughts, instead of listening. Arthur really motivated that manager *not* to buy from him, and that was the opposite of what Arthur wanted to do. A little listening could have made a lot of difference.

What Makes Some Employees Want to Quit

Ned B. was chief supervisor of a large department in a big-city bank. One day he received a report that one of his most valuable employees, Madge C., was quitting, and so he sent for her supervisor, George K., who explained that Madge was very angry and upset, and some of her resentment was directed at him, her supervisor. There had been a lot of extra work, some of it urgent, and quite a lot of absences; and Madge had been stuck with a lot of late work—which meant going home in the dark, alone, to a neighborhood where that might not be very safe. Lately, there had just been too much of this for Madge, and when the last bundle of work landed on her desk rather late, on the day before, she had "hit the ceiling." And Madge was too good an employee to lose.

"What did she say?" Ned asked the supervisor, who was not known to be a good listener.

"Well, you know—she just sounded off, like she has before;

and then, all of a sudden, she handed me her quitting notice. Just like that!''

"Just like that, eh? And she *has* sounded off before? There must be something else, George. Tell her I'd like to see her. Send her in here.''

When Madge C. came to Ned's desk a little later, Ned could see by the way she looked and held herself that she was "up tight''—tense, upset, overwrought. He did his best to put her at her ease and get her to relax.

How Listening to People Can Change Them

"Now, Madge,'' he said, gently, "please, as a favor to me, tell me what the problem is with you, before we lose any more valuable employees. Explain to me just what has happened that made you want to quit. Whatever happened, please be sure we couldn't have wanted it to happen the way it did, if it made you want to quit. So, please, tell me the whole story. I really want to know what happened.''

Madge began to talk, and Ned listened. He didn't interrupt at all. He nodded, he murmured sympathetic little murmurs in the right places to show he was really listening, and he gave her all his attention. His eyes were fixed on her; his body faced her; his face was turned fully on her. He sat upright, leaning a little toward her. He was obviously "all attention.'' When she paused, he just looked at her more intently, sometimes raising his eyebrows a little, or saying "yes?'' in an inquiring way—all to show as clearly as possible that *he was very much interested*, and to encourage her to keep talking.

When she began, she was emotional, excited; her pose was rigid; her voice was pitched high and strained; her tone was harsh. But gradually, as she went on, she eased, relaxed. Her voice became softer, her expression milder. She spoke more slowly.

Hers was a typical story of inadequate management: the capable, willing employee overloaded; the work that had to be done left to the few who could or would do it; faithful service, loyalty and cooperativeness abused and exploited under the necessity for handling volume and peak loads, and meeting deadlines.

Ned waited her out. He sat quietly, concentrating on her, letting her see that he was giving her all his attention, until she finally talked herself out and became silent; and even then he waited, before asking her if there was anything more she cared to tell him.

Then he thanked her for taking the trouble to tell him all this; and then he asked her if she wanted to hear what he thought about it. She did.

Explaining to Others Why People Act As They Do

"I wish you would try to understand George, Madge," he told her. "Poor fellow, he's badly off, too—and I suppose it's at least partly my fault. Here we have these special reports, and the regular quarterly summaries, all coming at once; along with more routine work than usual. And we *are* understaffed; and there *are* too many absences; and you know better than I the kind of help we are getting, nowadays; and how much you can depend on a lot of these kids just out of high school.

"George is very conscientious—and I know you will understand and even appreciate that about him. He accepts the responsibility for getting the job done; but he can't possibly do it all himself—though I believe he would if he could! So he must look to those he knows can really help. He'll be in even tougher shape without you, of course; and I don't blame you for thinking it's all his own fault. But in a way, Madge, he really couldn't help it."

Madge acknowledged all this, but made it clear she couldn't and wouldn't put up with any more of being required to work late. And that was just what Ned had been waiting to hear.

"Well, Madge," he asked her, "suppose you knew that you would never have to work past six o'clock. Would that take care of the situation? If George gives you a guarantee that he'll chase you out of there by six, even if you want to stay? How would you feel about that?" Ned's listening paid off.

Madge didn't yield immediately, but soon Ned was able to hand her George's report of her quitting; telling her to save it, to use if George ever violated the agreement. Ned had saved a valuable employee. He had motivated her to withdraw her resignation, and to stay.

How a Supervisor Persuaded a Good Worker Not to Quit

Ned B. was able to motivate Madge C., really, by listening to her. He knew she was in no condition to listen to him, and that he would have to let her "blow off steam" before she could be expected to "listen to reason." Madge was almost a different person after "getting it all off her chest." Psychologists call this *catharsis*: people can actually talk away a lot of the emotional and passionate attitudes that keep *them* from listening.

What Ned finally said to Madge would have had little or no effect if Ned had started with it *before* listening; she was in no mood to listen to such an explanation; she would have been passionately stubborn about quitting. It was Ned's *listening* that put her in a more receptive mood.

Why Ned B. Was So Successful

In addition, it was only by listening to Madge very carefully that Ned was able to *learn*—and to learn *from her*—just *what to say*, and *how to say it*. If he hadn't listened carefully and understood, he might have said the wrong thing, even after Madge was ready to listen. That would *really* have blown it!

Listening worked in two different but parallel ways, to enable Ned to motivate Madge to change her mind about quitting, and agree to stay. Both of these were essential to his success.

First, by hearing her out, by showing her that he was interested in her, by making it clear that he was listening carefully, attentively, to *all* she had to say, he gave her the opportunity to "talk herself out"—and thus become willing to listen to him. He helped her to change from an attitude where motivation by him was impossible, to an attitude where his motivational tactics could be effective. Without this, nothing he could have said would have worked.

Second, by listening carefully he learned what to say and how to say it. He knew—from listening to her—how to respond in a way that would not again arouse her emotions. She was in a very sensitive state; a false move would have set her off again. He had to avoid this. Listening made this possible for him. Also, listening to her as he did gave him a special *standing* with Madge.

Understanding the Difference Between Listening and Hearing

Another word on listening: there is sometimes a difference between *listening* and *hearing*. Some people listen but do not hear. They do not "get" what is being said—usually because they are thinking their own thoughts instead of *really* listening. Too often, they are getting ready to say something themselves, while waiting for the other person to stop talking. Merely waiting for the other person to stop is not really *listening*—because you do not really *hear* what he is saying. And the other person can tell!

That was the trouble with George K.—he didn't really *hear* what Madge was saying when she complained repeatedly about overwork and late hours and going home in the dark. He was too busy thinking about his own problems. So, when she finally quit, he was surprised and annoyed. He shouldn't have been surprised. If he had really *listened* to her before, he would have *heard* that she was fed up, and wouldn't take it any more. He could have done something about that—IF he had only heard. Maybe he didn't hear because he didn't want to.

By failing to listen properly, George motivated Madge to quit. By listening skillfully, Ned motivated Madge to stay. THE FIRST RULE OF MOTIVATING OTHERS IS: *LISTEN!*

2. AN IMPORTANT SOURCE OF VITAL INFORMATION

When you want to motivate a person—that is, to affect his own motivations in such a way as to cause him to want to do what you want him to do—then you need all the help you can get to know and understand those motivations that you will have to deal with, and to know how you are doing. You will have to know or find out quite a few things about a person whose motivations you want to affect. In addition to your ears, your eyes can be a big help. You will need some cues that can tell you if you are on the right track or not; and your eyes can also pick up such cues.

How to Pick Up Important Cues

Remember now, that people act in accordance with their own psychological *needs*. Obviously, the more you know about such needs, the better chance you have to work upon and with them. Sometimes you can make a person realize that doing what you want them to do will satisfy a need for them, directly. At other times, you will have to figure out how to make them accept the idea that doing what you want them to do will have other results which will lead —however indirectly—to the satisfaction of one or more of their needs. In most such situations, your eyes can usually be a big help in picking up cues about those needs, and how your *leverage* about them is working.

Ed S. was a promising young executive in the Chicago office of a large manufacturing company. A conference of higher level executives had been discussing the installation of a computerized system at one of the company's plants in a small town in North Carolina, and it had been agreed that Ed should be sent out to take care of the matter personally. Ed was especially competent in this type of project, but his immediate superior was very doubtful that Ed would be willing to go.

"Ed likes it here in Chicago," he told the group. "He won't want to leave. He's a big city boy, and he has a lot of family and friends around here. I don't think I could persuade him to move to Croydonville."

He suggested that the vice-president in charge of manufacturing should be the one to try to talk Ed into going, since Ed would be reporting directly to him during his stay at the Croydonville plant. The v-p manufacturing, Lou T., was a canny soul, if a forceful one; and he agreed to take on the assignment of persuading Ed.

How Lou T. Picked Up and Used Some Important Cues

Instead of sending for Ed, or having Ed's boss send him, Lou telephoned, and arranged to come to Ed's own office. When he came in, he took advantage of the opening moments of greetings and pleasantries to look around. He noticed a picture of a nice-looking young woman with three children who seemed to be about seven, ten and thirteen years old.

He asked about the picture, and Ed was pleased to tell about his wife, Madeleine; his boys—Pete, and Ed, junior; and his daughter Josephine.

Lou's eyes also took notice of a few other personal items on display in Ed's office; and then he was ready to start on his job of persuading Ed to move to Croydonville.

"Ed," he began, "there's a big opportunity opening up, and the Executive Committee has already agreed that you're the best man for it. You'd be reporting to me, and I've asked for you, so you can see that it could be very good for your career. And I think it would be very good for Pete and for Ed Junior, and for Josephine; and I've a hunch that Madeleine might like it, too.

"And I see you're quite a golfer." (Lou had spotted a couple of golf trophies in Ed's office.) "Well, where we all want you to go you will be playing golf all year 'round—even all winter; and the golf course is only ten minutes from the plant, so you can get in at least nine holes every day after work."

Lou had also noticed a picture of a small cabin cruiser, with all of Ed's family in it, holding fishing rods. So he went on: "The company will send your boat on down there, for you. There's a real big lake, with all kinds of fish; you can boat and fish all year, and you can swim all year except maybe a couple of months.

"And there's a real good school—ask Tom P., you know him. He's had his family down there, and maybe you can get the house he had, or one like it—big enough, real comfortable, and with grounds big enough for catch, and tag, or even touch-football.

"I'm talking about Croydonville, Ed; we need you down there to see that the new computerized system goes in right. If you do a good job down there—and I know you will—there'll be a bigger job for you back here, in a year or two. Now, how about it?"

Ed couldn't turn that down cold—Lou had aimed his pitch at too many of Ed's needs. He asked a lot of questions.

Lou listened carefully and gave honest, straightforward answers; but he shaped and adapted them to what he already knew about Ed, and what more he could learn from the questions Ed asked.

Finally, when Lou felt he had said about all that needed to be said at that time, he rose.

"Well, Ed, I suppose you'll want to kick it around with your Madeleine, and maybe with the kids, too," he concluded. "Just remember—it's good for your career, and it'll be good for your family, and for you. Feel free to get back to me any time, if you need to know any more. The company will cover all out-of-pocket expenses, of course; and there ought to be a raise coming your way as soon as we see how you take hold down there. It'll be a pleasure for me to have you on my team. I know the boys at Croydonville will be truly glad to have you down there to help them get set up right; and you'll really enjoy it down there. See you!"

Ed S. had heard rumors about the Croydonville project; and he had privately decided that if it came his way he didn't want it, because he didn't want to move. But he really hadn't thought of all the other advantages Lou had brought up; and it was these that made the difference—to Ed and to his family.

How *Cues* Can Help Determine Your *Target Plan*

Lou was able to target his shots so neatly because he kept his eyes open. And they actually told him how to move. He knew how to use the *advantages* he had, but they would not have been enough. His eyes made the difference. They spotted the values, the interests, the "needs" that could really motivate Ed. If Lou hadn't looked at those pictures in Ed's office, he might have missed out on some really important cues.

Your eyes can tell you many things, if you use them, that can help you to motivate people more effectively. Sometimes they can tell you when to stop and pull back, before you get into a position that you wouldn't be able to back out of.

How to Interpret Some Important Cues

For instance, if you see that the *target individual* keeps looking away, doesn't want to look at you, this is a pretty clear indication that there is something on the person's mind that he'd rather not talk about. If that is happening, and if you push too hard, the "No!" you get could be the last word. That is probably the signal to hold everything, try to break off tactfully, and then try to figure out what the obstacles might be, and how to meet and overcome them, before you try again.

You may see the *target individual* suddenly fold his arms across his chest and lean back. That is usually a sign of resistance; even of rejection of what you are saying. If you keep on in the same way, you will probably head into a stubborn negative. Back away, smooth the situation, and try again some other time, after you have worked out a better approach.

On the other hand, you can get encouraging, confirmatory "feedback" from the person you are working on; "feedback" that will tell you when you are on the right track; when to press a point that really fits. Most people are not very "deadpan": if you make a good point they usually show some sign—perhaps a nod, or a tilting of the head, or even the lifting of a frown, or the glimpse of a smile.

Be alert for cues like these. They tell you that you have a green light for your present course and that you are getting a positive, interested reaction. Keep watching as you press home with the line that your eyes tell you is aimed right at a need. That is your cue to motivate!

3. DISCOVERING WHAT IS REALLY IMPORTANT

When you listen and look carefully, you will hear and see a great deal. Much of this may be interesting, and some of it can tempt you to an immediate follow-up. But if you are really trying to motivate someone, to work upon someone's psychological or other "needs" in order for them to be motivated along the lines that you desire, it is important to work according to your *motivation plan*—on the ideas and incentives that really count for your purpose. And that means you shouldn't get too involved with other ideas that do not count very much for what you want to accomplish.

Finding Out Which of the *Target Individual's* Needs Are Important (to *Him!*) and Which Are Not!

Once you determine the "needs" you are going to work on, the others become unimportant for your purposes. Don't forget them; but set them aside, to be worked on later if your experience indicates you should work on these also. Anything that concerns the "target needs" will be relevant. Anything else is now irrelevant. To concentrate on the relevant, you will have to identify and set aside the irrelevant.

Neil K. was a clerk in the accounting department at Rossman Corporation, a large wholesale groceries distributor. He was performing satisfactorily; and his supervisor, Norm G., felt that he had the potential to take over the cashier's cage when the present senior cashier retired in about a year. But Neil wasn't interested.

Norm had talked to him about it several times, pointing out that Neil would first have to learn some new techniques, as well as become familiar with the forms, machines, methods and procedures, and the system generally. But Neil hadn't even begun; and time was going by.

Finally, one day Norm sent for Neil, determined to settle the matter. He asked Neil to sit down, inquired about his family, complimented him on a small, rather routine assignment he had completed, and then got down to the business at hand.

"Look, Neil," he began. "You know Bob retires next October. You know that I'd like to see you take over. I know you can do it. That could mean a nice raise for you; and I'm sure you could use it.

"But whoever takes over has to be able to run the job. There are six youngsters in there, and most of them need help a lot of the time. I'll help you all I can. Bob will show you the ropes; I've arranged with him to stay a couple of hours past closing, at least one night a week, and I'll do the same. And there's a course at the University Extension you ought to take—that's on Thursday evenings—which starts next month. So you see, everything is all set for you. And, of course, I'll expect you to coach young Haskins to take over your desk."

Understanding How People Avoid Giving Reasons Why They Act As They Do

Neil looked downward and away. He slouched in his seat. He didn't say anything for a moment; then he looked up, but away, out of the window. Finally he spoke.

"I don't know, Norm. I'll have to think about it."

"*Think* about it?" Norm returned, explosively. "For the sweet love of Pete—what's the matter? You've been here eight years now. You've been in your present job four of those years. Don't you want to get ahead, man? Here I'm offering you a promotion, and a raise; a chance to move upward a good step toward *my* job, some day. What is there to *think* about, Neil? What's the matter with you?"

Neil certainly showed that he didn't want to answer, but he couldn't very well avoid making some reply. Clearly, he was troubled; but he finally came up with an explanation.

"It's all those evenings, Norm. Going to class, and staying late with you and Bob, and all that. I'd be home late two or three times a week. Jane wouldn't go for that!"

"You mean to tell me that if you explained to Jane why you were going to be home late—to get a better job, a promotion and a raise—she wouldn't go along with that?"

How to Tell When People Give the Wrong Reasons

"That's the way it is, Norm. She likes me to be home for dinner with her and the kids. I couldn't fight that."

Norm couldn't believe all that; and the interview broke up on that note. Norm was disgusted with Neil, but he was also frustrated; he really had no other likely candidate for the replacement; and he knew Neil would be a good man for the job. He just couldn't understand Neil's refusal to give up some evenings in order to qualify. There must be something wrong there, he thought.

Norm gave the whole matter quite a lot of thought. And then, after a week, he sent for Neil again.

"OK, Neil, I've fixed things up so you can get organized for Bob's job without staying evenings. We'll free you up from your regular work two mornings a week. One you'll spend with Bob, and one with me. And here's a book—it's the text for that course at the Extension. Bob and I figure that if you really study this book, and work with us, you'll be OK!"

But Neil was still not sold. He fidgeted, he looked out of the window, he frowned; he was obviously very uneasy, but he didn't say anything. Norm couldn't understand the situation. Here he'd gone to all this length to meet Neil's crazy objection to giving up his evenings, and still Neil wasn't content.

"What is it, Neil?" he demanded, but quietly. "You'd better tell me! I know now that it isn't just those evenings. There's something else holding you back. Better spill it—now!"

Neil was terribly embarrassed, but he still wouldn't agree to do what Norm wanted. Norm realized, then, that Neil's objection to giving up his evenings was not a real objection. It was irrelevant. The real reason was something else. Someday, maybe, Norm would find out. Neil didn't offer any other explanation; he simply asked Norm to forget the whole thing. Norm became rather angry, and that was that.

How the Real Reasons Can Usually Be Figured Out

Three months later Neil came to Norm, and asked if there was still an opportunity for him to understudy for that promotion. Now he was willing to work hard on it—evenings included! Norm, who had planned to advertise for a replacement, finally agreed; and Neil immediately began to show a real determination to prove his ability to master the cashier's cage operations.

But Norm was truly puzzled. What could have changed Neil's mind? He tried to think of everything that had happened just before Neil's change of heart—anything that could possibly shed some light on the problem.

And then—suddenly—he had it. One of the young assistants in the cashier's cage, a rather attractive but also rather flighty girl, had quit just the week before Neil had come in with his surprising change of heart. Norm put two and two together, remembering some incidents at an office party and a few other details. Neil, it seems, had gotten himself somewhat involved with that girl —enough to make it too embarrassing—and potentially too explosive—for him to risk becoming her boss. But once she was gone, the way was clear for Neil to do just as Norm wanted.

The reasons Neil gave to Norm were irrelevant. He indicated needs, and Norm met them; but they were irrelevant. The real obstacle was never identified—until after it had disappeared. Norm had suspected that there was something peculiar about Neil's objections; but he had accepted them, and acted on them. If he had listened—and looked—more, and more carefully, he might have put two and two together a lot sooner. The cues had been there all the time!

People who are resisting persuasion commonly offer objections that are spurious—not the real ones, which they may have reason to wish to conceal. Instead they may talk about needs of theirs that are now being met, but which the suggested change might no longer allow to be met. They are trying to conceal their real motivations by suggesting others that are not the real ones. Such tactics are intended to protect the *status quo*; and the real reasons for resisting a proposed change may be entirely different.

If you are trying to motivate someone, and meet some resistance, be sure you operate on the real needs; and do not let yourself be led astray by any that may be non-existent or irrelevant.

4. TESTING FOR THE TRUTH

In the previous section we saw how a supervisor (Norm) was taken in by considerations (reasons, excuses, etc.) presented by an employee (Neil) that were not really relevant. As a result, he spent quite a lot of time and effort trying to solve the wrong problem. In that case, the man was really motivated to do as the supervisor wanted, but was prevented by a stronger motivation not to do as both he and the supervisor wanted.

To motivate people successfully, you must deal with their real needs; their real interests; their real motivations. You must learn to recognize what is really relevant to your *motivation plan*—what *must* be considered.

Life is full of false and misleading excuses and reasons, which people offer to conceal their true motivations—or, at least, the real reasons why they act as they do. For example, just take the simple matter of lunch. An acquaintance to whom you suggest lunching together says he (or she) is too busy, or never eats anything but a sandwich, or never goes out, or has another appointment, or whatnot.

How People Mean—Or Feel—Differently Than What They Say

Any of these reasons or excuses for turning you down may be true, but they may also be offered to conceal the truth; and the truth may, of course, be anything from their need to save money, to their lack of interest in your company, or even to a fear that they may get stuck with the whole check. It may even be a combination of some or all of these, or other factors you cannot know.

One way to "zero in" on the truth is to check, or test. The supervisor in the previously related case actually did this, in a way, when he met the clerk's objections by arranging to eliminate the evenings of preparation. Then it turned out that these were not the real objections, which still existed. Meeting or removing stated obstacles or objections should eliminate resistance—if the obstacles or objections stated were real. If resistance continues, obviously there are other reasons, which may leave you just about where you were. In the previous case, for instance, the *real* barrier was recognized only after it had been eliminated by accident.

How to Test for the Truth by "Gaming"

One of the techniques you can use to test relevancy is by "gaming." This means involving the person you are trying to motivate in an "as if" situation. By playing this game skillfully, you can often learn if the "need" you are working on is indeed an adequately motivational one; or if there is some obstacle to the ways or means by which the goal is to be reached. The game can be played in a "let's suppose" mode; or the whole thing can be managed within the framework of something like: "I've got a problem, and I'd appreciate it if you'd let me talk it over with you—you might have an idea for me." That way, you may be able to make the *target individual* really tell you what you need to know.

Jay B., a district sales-manager, wanted to persuade Peter S., one of his best salesmen, to change territories with Bob N., a new man. Peter was particularly good at opening up new accounts. Bob was not nearly so good at this, but was excellent at servicing accounts once they were opened up. Peter was resisting the switch. He said he liked his territory, he had a lot of friends there, and had good relations with his accounts; and anyhow he lived in the territory and it was very convenient and handy for him to stay there.

Jay brought Peter into the office at the end of a selling day, and they went out for a long talk over a cocktail or two. Jay brought along a pad of paper and some sharp pencils.

After a friendly warm-up, Jay started his "game."

"Pete," he began, "I'd like your help in getting a better idea of what the situation really is, or could be. What do you really think of the sales potential in Bob's territory? His accounts bring in an average of only about $6,000 gross sales a month, now. You know something about that territory—you covered it for Bob during his vacation, and for the other men there in the years before that. What do you think a good man could do with it, in say, six months or a year?"

"Well, Jay, of course you could never be certain; but there's a lot of potential there that Bob hasn't been able to tap. There's really a lot of volume in products like ours going to the competition. We ought to be able to take over quite a bit of that, especially if our man knew how to sell the advantages of the new line. No question, the territory ought to bring in a lot more."

"Your territory is up around $12,000 a month—one of our best. Do you think Bob's could ever do as well?"

"Well, maybe, after a year or two. It certainly ought to go up to $10,000 or more pretty soon. More, later. Actually, there isn't any reason why Bob's territory shouldn't be as productive as any, if it were handled right."

"OK; thanks, Peter. That's what I thought. Now, you know I have a problem. I think Bob is real good at servicing accounts; but he just hasn't learned yet how to land new ones. I want to put Bob in a well-developed territory, where he ought to be able to hold everything we have now, at least, and learn. And I want to put a real go-getter in the territory that Bob has now—someone who can really build it up. I only have a few good men I could use. Now, Pete, what do you think I'd have to offer to get one of them to switch territories?"

Getting the Facts that Count

"Well, naturally, Jay, they wouldn't want to lose out by it, would they? They'd want to keep on making as much as they are now, with a chance to make more if they do the job you expect. And another thing—there'd be a heavy expense out of the man's pocket for entertainment and all that, working on new accounts; and maybe the cost of a longer trip to and from the territory from wherever the man lives now. He'd want to feel he was getting ahead, not falling behind."

Now Jay realized what Pete's "needs" were. Pete himself had just made them clear. He had never stated his objections so frankly, before. The ones he had offered were, in fact, irrelevant.

"I see," Jay nodded. "And I think you're right, too, Pete, So let's see what I could do. Suppose I take a man from a territory like yours, grossing $12,000 a month. At 15% commission, that's $1800 a month. Bob's take is about $900 a month now. Hmm. Let me think a minute. If I gave Bob 7½%, instead of 15%, on the accounts he takes over in a $12,000 territory, that would be $900 —just about what he gets now; and that would leave $900 for the man that built up that territory, to add to the $900 from Bob's territory—there's the $1800 he had. And I could give him a special allowance, for a year, say, for expenses—entertainment and extra travel. And every new account he sold would bring him 15% more, on top. If he built that new territory up to $12,000 he'd be getting another $900—that would make $2700 a month. And that's more than anybody else takes home, in this district. How do you think that would work, Pete?"

Pete looked at him, with a certain smile.

"I think you're one dangerous guy to drink with. When do I

start breaking Bob in on my territory?''

How to Bring Out the Real Attitudes

Jay's "game" had brought out Pete's genuine feelings about the situation: the way he really evaluated the possibilities, and the way he saw the incentives necessary to make the switch attractive. And so then Jay knew how to offer Pete just what was needed to motivate him to do what Jay wanted him to do.

Looking at the situation before their "game," Pete had simply seen the obstacles and objections. He hadn't really thought of what Jay might do—would have to do—to get a "yes" out of him. The "game" clarified his own thoughts, brought the right kind of inducement to bear, and helped him to say "yes!" to Pete. For both Pete and Jay, the "game" brought out what was relevant, and so made it possible for the motivation to succeed.

How to Avoid Deceiving Ourselves by "Projecting"

Determining what is absolutely relevant is of primary importance in planning for the motivation of others. Guessing at the psychological "needs" of others can easily lead one astray, since no two people are alike, and everyone is tempted to assume that others think and feel as they do.

Psychologists use the word "projection" for the psychological mechanism by which we "project" onto (attribute to) others the ideas, needs, feelings, thoughts, purposes, motivations, etc. which we have ourselves. But we cannot, of course, look directly into another's mind; we tend, instead, to look into our own, and to deceive ourselves into believing that what we have there exists in the other person.

Because of this tendency to "project," we must be very careful about assuming anything about other people's needs, thoughts, feelings, motives, etc. Those who say they "can tell what another person is thinking" are really deceiving themselves; they can only know what they themselves *believe* the other is thinking; and they can be very wrong.

But we do have to try to understand what makes other people "tick." Before we can work on their motivations, we have to understand what their needs are, and what will satisfy them. And so we must try to judge from their actual behavior; from *some* of the things they say; and from some of the things we know about them. And then, when we have put together what we believe is a sound working basis for motivation, we should test, check, try it out, in order to make sure that we are working on what is relevant.

5. HOW TO COMBINE THE IMPORTANT ELEMENTS TO GAIN MOTIVATIONAL LEVERAGE

Most people you deal with have more intelligence than they generally show. You should always distinguish between *knowledge* and *intelligence*. Knowledge one acquires, possesses, and may forget. Knowledge can be learned. It has far more to do with environment or opportunity or experience than intelligence does; knowledge comes to us from the outside.

But intelligence is something else again. Intelligence has a lot to do with the way we *use* our knowledge—what we *do* with what we know. Some people are what Harry Truman called "educated damn' fools"—they may know a lot, but they act in a way that suggests they have poor judgment. So far as their significant behavior goes, in many situations, "they might as well be ignorant."

On the other hand, we constantly see people who may have had few educational advantages, and whose special knowledge or even general knowledge may be deficient, but who somehow, in a given situation, act with shrewdness, good judgment, insight and cleverness to come up with what is, for them, the most advantageous possible action. Sometimes we are amazed and surprised at the resourcefulness, creativity and imagination shown by a decision or an apparent course of action taken by a person who has always appeared to be extremely "limited."

How People Act in What They *Think* Is Their Own Best Interest

Whatever else this may mean to us—and it can and should mean a lot—it surely signifies that most people can easily tell what they *believe* is in their own best interest. They can be wrong, of course; they can be guilty of serious misevaluations; but they can usually develop, rather rapidly and assuredly, a reaction about how any development or proposal affects or relates to their own interests—as *they* see these.

If people like this are to be motivated—and most people are basically like this—the major problem in motivating them is to set up a situation, actual or proposed, in which they will see a *desired* benefit to themselves. If this can be done, the communication problem is not usually a serious one—most people will "catch on" right away; they will see and recognize the implications for themselves, and react quite swiftly and clearly (to themselves).

How a Benefit to *A* Is Not Necessarily a Benefit to *B*

Note the qualification in the paragraph above: a *desired* benefit. They must *themselves* desire the suggested benefit. What one person may think to be advantageous to another may, in the event, be regarded as of little interest, or even as the reverse of advantageous.

A common example is found, in Great Britain, in the offering of peerages to some important persons. This traditional "honor," ostensibly from the sovereign, but actually from the Parliamentary party in power, has been a traditional goal of many distinguished figures. Yet some reject it. They do so because they believe a title will not go well with their public image; or because it will "elevate" them to the House of Lords, and so prevent them from serving in the far more important Commons; or for some other reason. In any event, the government ministers who desire to motivate someone by making him a Lord may be assuming a value for a lordship that is not shared by the individual to whom it is offered. The incentive simply does not have, for the one who rejects it, the significance, value, or motivational effect that it is believed to have by those who offer it. For them, it is *not* a benefit.

The Two Elements That Can Produce the Results You Want

From this you can see the necessity for connecting the two elements that are essential for bringing about a motivational effect: the desire, and the benefit that meets this; the psychological need, and the satisfier; the want, and the fulfillment; the susceptibility or vulnerability, and the values or experience that meets these.

In the Mohammedan Caliphate of a few hundred years ago in the Near East, corruption was often a way of life; and anyone who wanted anything from the governing officials knew they had to resort to bribery to motivate those in power to do as they wished.

There was a saying, then, that summed up the principle of offering to each individual the kind of bribe to which he would be most receptive: "To a pasha (military leader), women; to a palace eunuch, gold!" No doubt a bribe of gold also could have motivated a pasha; but this adage made the resounding point that there was no possible advantage in offering an inducement that could have no value for the individual to be influenced. It could have little *leverage*.

The motivating factor can exist in the desired course of action, itself. Or the desired course of action may have to be motivated by external added factors. Thus an honest official is motivated by the desire to do his duty; the dishonest official may expect a bribe before he does what he is supposed to do.

The difference is illustrated clearly in the contrast between a) a man and woman who are in love with one another, and find the motivation for their love-making in the joys and pleasures they find in their mutual indulgence; or b) the hiring of a prostitute. The experience of physical intimacy is no attraction for the prostitute; she must be motivated to indulge the man by the *leverage* of money, which has otherwise nothing to do with the course of action he demands of her.

Motivating from the Inside or the Outside

Thus we are concerned with the difference between *inherent* motivation, where the process of acting as desired brings its own reward; and *extraneous* (outside) motivation, where the motivational element must be introduced from outside and when it is usually regarded as an "incentive."

The payment of wages or salaries for the performance of work is the most common extraneous motivator. But some persons find such satisfaction in their work that they are motivated to do it far better than they would for pay alone. Pay is regarded as an incentive; and, as such, it is the basic motivator for most employees, though some may speak of how much they enjoy their work.

Whether the motivational factor is inherent or extraneous, it must be well-enough adapted to a psychological need, or it will not have the intended effect. For a person who really *needs* a job, pay may be a primary motivation. For a financially independent person, the nature of the work and its inherent satisfactions become the major consideration. But even the person who most needs the pay will also be conscious of the qualities of the job—the frustrations and annoyances, the satisfactions and gratifications, the irritations and abuses, the incidental enjoyments and pleasures.

Developing Better Awareness of What People Like or Dislike

It is important, in a continuing relationship, to observe keenly the "positives" and "negatives" of an individual's interactions in a continuing situation. For instance, a supervisor should maintain constant awareness of how his people react to circumstances and developments—even to suggestions and possibilities. In this way, he can develop a knowledge of what will be liked and what will be disliked; what will be tolerated and what will be preferred; what will be ignored and what will be appreciated; and what will be worth a great deal in terms of personal contribution, effort, attitude, acceptance, etc.

Armed with this kind of knowledge and understanding of individuals, the supervisor can design his "motivatings" appropriately for those with whom he has to deal, and for his own purposes. He can bring to bear the most effective motivators for the particular person and purpose. He can connect the significant need with the significant satisfaction. He can match hope with promise, aspiration with prospect, desire with fulfillment. He can tailor the "can have" to the "want." And he will be able to avoid dangling the wrong bait, offering the wrong inducement, holding out the compensation that would not compensate.

This is not always easy to do, but only the supervisor who thinks about his people will know what will motivate them; only the salesman who really listens to his customers will know how to handle them; only the negotiator who has studied his man will know what kind of offer or proposal to make.

The relevant motivator must be matched to the relevant susceptibility—the satisfaction to the need. A valuable employee who is thinking of quitting may be motivated to stay on by a friendly lunch and a pat on the back—or by a big raise and promises of promotion. A prospect may sign an order for a big discount and assurances of special additional services—or for a simple personal promise of satisfaction. A child may strive for good marks at school to please a parent—or for an expensive reward. A person may react favorably to a small immediate reward, and be unmoved by the offer of a far greater reward in the future. (Future pensions often have little appeal for the young.) People react differently to the motivators of money, friendship, praise, achievement and all the other satisfactions or means of securing satisfactions. This is because people have very different needs and combinations of needs, and these change with changing conditions.

The successful motivator understands all this. He takes the time and trouble to identify needs that are important enough to the individual, and to connect these up with motivational factors that not only fit those needs, but are practical and appropriate under the circumstances.

7

HOW TO WIN
LOYALTY AND SUPPORT
WITH MOTIVATIONAL LEVERAGE

In many situations, existing disagreement is an important factor. You may want to get people to agree with you, or to agree with one another, or to do what you want them to do in spite of disagreement with you or with others. This chapter suggests how Motivational Leverage can help you, even in such difficult situations.

1. HOW TO USE AGREEMENT
TO AROUSE SUPPORT

Before you can plan to motivate someone, you need to know something about them. You need especially to know something about their values—what they like and do not like; and you need to know how much agreement or disagreement there is between you and them. One of the most important ways of finding out what you need to know is by testing.

People are almost always easier to motivate if they sense that there is agreement between you and them. On the other hand, they are often very difficult to motivate if they do not feel that you are in agreement with them, and they with you. And even if you and they are not in complete agreement, you can often find enough basis for agreement to make motivation feasible.

How to Test for Areas of Agreement that Will Help You

In order to find as much agreement as possible, or at least as much as needed to be effective, you often have to do some testing. This kind of testing is aimed at finding and exploring the areas of agreement, so that these can be emphasized. It may even be necessary to find and explore the areas of disagreement, so these can be minimized. Once you have successfully tested the basis for agreement, you can go ahead and use this effectively to motivate the person or persons with whom the agreement exists.

Sizing Up the Degrees of Agreement, to Pick the Stronger

At first thought it might seem that "agreement is agreement"—that if you agree with someone, that is all there is to it. However, there is a great deal more to it than that. There is a vast range of agreement behavior, from the meaningless, automatic chiming in of the "yes-man" to the rapturous and unique self-dedication of "I do!" in the true-love wedding.

There is the grudging "yes—but—." And there is the downgrading "ye-e-e-es—of course"—(meaning "*everybody* knows *that*"); and the enthusiastic "*yes!*—of *course!*"—spoken in a very different way (meaning "yes!—*emphatically yes!*"). There is the formula "Right on!" and the million ways of saying "O.K." There are any number of ways of nodding the head, that can express, along with assent, anything from reverence to impatience. There is the "Amen!" that implies fervent agreement; and the offhand "I suppose so!" that suggests you couldn't care less, and don't really go along. And so it goes—on and on and on.

It seems to be a law of nature that people tend to be motivated favorably toward those with whom they are in agreement, or whom they believe to be in agreement with themselves. Obviously, the stronger the agreement, the more favorable the effect should be.

How Agreement Can Improve Your *Standing* and Your *Advantages*

While there are interesting occasional exceptions, it is wise to consider that agreement can be a useful means to develop and to improve *standing* with the individual to be motivated. Agreement can also play a decisive part by linking you to an important *target motivation*, or by expressing or improving your *advantage*.

For such reasons as these, it is desirable to maximize and to optimize agreement with the individual you seek to motivate; that is, to develop agreement both quantitatively and qualitatively. This means that you find as many areas of agreement as possible (subject to the limitation of basic honesty); and that you manifest or express these agreements in the most appropriate and effective ways.

This certainly does not mean that you should try for or offer blind, slavish agreement on everything. Anyone who carries agreement that far stands a pretty good chance—with intelligent, responsible people—of losing their respect to such an extent that his *standing* will be severely limited. They may accept and be gratified by his toadying; but they are unlikely to feel that such behavior indicates strength of character, high intelligence, great capacity, or even basic honesty.

How You Can Benefit by Maximizing Agreement

However, it is usually possible to maximize areas of agreement without surrendering or impairing self-respect or dignity, and without forfeiting the regard of others. In fact, if it is seen that you go out of your way to find areas of agreement—while still reserving your own views of some matters—it is rather likely to raise your *standing* all around.

Johnny B. wants his boss to promote him. He wants to motivate the boss to do this. But the boss thinks Johnny is too young. And Johnny can't agree to that! But Johnny goes ahead, anyhow, to test areas of agreement. Leave age out of it. What does the boss *really* want?

Take some of the more essential considerations. Experience? Knowledge? Reliability? Can they agree on matters like these? How does the boss feel about Johnny's experience? What has Johnny learned? Is Johnny reliable?

Johnny can work on getting the boss's agreement on these important components. If he succeeds, there will be more agreement than disagreement; and then perhaps the boss will be motivated to overlook the inadequate (?) number of years that Johnny has lived, and give him the promotion, anyhow, on the strength of the areas of agreement.

Al T., a real estate agent, wants to sell a house to the Pinkhams. They think it is too large and costs too much; but they admit it is handsome and in a good neighborhood. Al, of course, emphasizes the areas of agreement: of course, it *is* handsome; it *is* in a good neighborhood.

But Al cannot agree that it is too large, or costs too much; so he works on these areas of disagreement, to find agreement.

Too large? But doesn't Mr. P. want a den? Won't Mrs. P.'s relatives be visiting? Won't a four-bedroom home in *this* neighborhood, where houses tend to be larger, have a better resale value? When he gets the P.'s to agree on those points, their objection that the house is too large loses most of its weight.

Costs too much? But look at the mortgage available; look at the resale value; look at it as an investment. Again, the P.'s have to agree with Al on these important considerations.

Al has a pretty good chance of motivating the Pinkhams to buy the house, once he has "engineered" the areas of disagreement into some of their components, and worked on building agreement. And he learned what he had to do by testing.

This is a basic mechanism for the motivation of others.

How Common Interests Increase Motivational Leverage

It is truly remarkable how much more readily people can be motivated by those with whom they feel they have a common interest. Sometimes even a trivial or completely irrelevant common interest can make a lot of difference. For instance, suppose you are trying to sell some life insurance to Ed G., who happens to be a real nut about professional football. If you can't talk professional football with Ed G., you have a real handicap, because he will think there is something peculiar about you. On the other hand, if you can engage in a good, satisfying give-and-take with Ed on his favorite subject, you will gain a lot of *standing* with him.

Suppose you disagree with Ed about some of his most cherished beliefs—which team or coach or ball carrier is "best," for instance; he will surely question your judgment. However, if you happen to have the same interest, and therefore you agree with him—not just to be agreeable, but intelligently, constructively, and on the basis of being well informed—Ed will not only welcome your support, but will also feel a lot of respect for your judgment, and confidence in you as a person. That can do a lot for your *leverage* with Ed. It could really warm things up.

It really pays to find out a lot about the interests and beliefs of any *target individual*. If you find or put yourself in a good position to demonstrate a true common interest, you will be well on your way to building the *leverage* you need.

2. HOW TO DISAGREE WITH PEOPLE AND STILL KEEP THEIR LOYALTY

It has often been said that disagreement is a real test of character. Remember: that means it is a test of *your* character, as well as that of anyone who disagrees with you.

It is easy to dislike people with whom we disagree. When we allow disagreement to become emotional, we tend to think of the opposition as being stupid, "blind to facts," mulishly stubborn, or insincere—even dishonest. When we feel that way about an individual, it is impossible for him to motivate us as he would wish. And if he feels that way about us, it is equally impossible for us to motivate him in any way we would like. So if we want to motivate someone favorably, it is very important not to get into a locked-horns, "I'm right—you're wrong" disagreement.

Disagreement tends to motivate us to avoid those with whom we disagree—to get away and keep away from them, just as the many religious and political dissenters fled Europe in the past and came to America to get away from disagreement and persecution. Disagreement may even motivate us to hostility. Politics and religion and race breed strong opinions, and strong feelings. They have been major causes of wars, rebellions, riots, civil disturbances, persecution, mob action and other forms of violence and agression.

How to Keep Disagreement from Motivating People the Wrong Way

Obviously, strong disagreement can motivate people very unfavorably, and it must be avoided. In some officers' messes, for instance, it has been a rule to avoid discussions of politics, religion—and women!

Deeply felt disagreement brings the danger of negative motivation—of motivating people to do something we do not want them to do. When we disagree deeply with someone, we tend to feel hostility toward them, which may take the form of avoidance, or of aggression. The more involved and concerned we are about the subject of our disagreement, the more intense the reaction of hostility is likely to be.

"Civilized," polite, well-bred people may conceal such adverse reactions; but they feel them, nonetheless. Disagreement represents a kind of threat. When someone disagrees with us, we feel that we may be wrong; and the more important the subject may be to us, the less willing we are to feel that we are wrong about it. Something we value may be valueless; something we count on as true may be false; something we have believed to be false may be true; some idea with which we have allied our egos may let us in for a fall. Under such circumstances, some people are motivated in strange ways that often seem quite illogical, even spiteful.

How Disagreement on One Subject Can Affect
Agreement on a Very Different Subject

Ross J. is a fanatical supporter of a certain professional football team which we may call the Locomotives. He is convinced they will win the championship, and he follows the news of the team with dedication. He is also Deputy Superintendent of a State Hospital.

One day, at lunch at the officers' table in the hospital cafeteria, Ross was speaking enthusiastically about the prowess and prospects of the Locomotives. Sitting across from him was a young newcomer, Todd L., recently hired as Assistant Manager of the Accounting Department. He listened to Ross with scarcely concealed impatience.

"Oh, I don't know!" he finally broke in. "I'm not so sure about that! How about the Charioteers? They beat the Hustlers by 38 to 22, while the Locomotices only won by 11 to 8. And look at what they did to the Bulldozers! My money's on the Charioteers!"

A few weeks later Todd was in Ross' office asking for the transfer of a senior clerk from Records to Accounting. As Ross sat listening to Todd's request, he could scarcely keep from thinking of him as the idiot who preferred the Charioteers to the Locomotives; which really meant that Todd had been proclaiming him, Ross, to be radically, fatally, irreversibly and eternally wrong—and that, about a subject of major importance!

No matter how fair Ross might try to be, this kind of reflection on Todd's character could not help but influence Ross against Todd when he considered the problems involved in transferring that senior clerk from Records to Accounting. So a disagreement about a football team kept Todd from motivating Ross to transfer that clerk. It hurt his *standing;* and it kept him from developing any *leverage* with that *target individual.*

It is surprising—almost unbelievable—how disagreements about Subject A can adversely affect agreements on Subject B, even when Subject A is quite irrelevant and unrelated to Subject B; and even when Subject A has nothing to do with anything affecting the appropriate relationship between the parties, while Subject B is closely related. In the example above, professional football had no possible connection with employee transfers or with the Accounting Department at the State Hospital; yet a personal disagreement about professional football teams had a very real effect upon a decision on an employee transfer affecting the Accounting Department.

How to Protect Your *Standing*

The handling of disagreement has a vital effect upon *standing*—the way the person who wants to motivate is seen (perceived) by the person to be motivated. The way you are seen or "perceived" by another person has a very important effect upon your chances to motivate him.

Sometimes the person to be motivated has a *self-image* so wrapped up in himself, so sensitive to disagreement and so intolerant of other views that only slavish "yessing" will keep him friendly and favorably disposed. If that is so, then whoever wants to motivate such a person must take this situation into account, and decide if the whole project is really worth the kowtowing and servility that it will require. Keeping your own self-respect, and earning the respect of those who understand the situation may be better for you, and for your *standing,* in the long run.

Perhaps there is another, better way to achieve the objective —anything from a direct confrontation to an "end run," or perhaps a bypass—such as finding a different *target individual* to accomplish the desired results. But if the objective is important, and if adequate *standing* with such a person is indispensable, then, by definition, there is no substitute for being as agreeable as necessary—whatever it takes.

How to Handle Disagreement Successfully

On the other hand, there are—fortunately—plenty of examples of people who are conscious of disagreement with one another on one issue or another, but who still manage to get along very well together, and to cooperate effectively where it counts: that is, where their interests and duties coincide. Voltaire said: "I despise what you say, but I will defend with my life your right to say it." To some fair-minded people, this principle is more important than any individual's opinion.

If the person to be motivated is at all "fair-minded"—capable of some degree of objectivity—then the effective tactic is to *play down* any subjects of disagreement and emphasize the area(s) of common interest. In such situations, the approaches suggested in the previous section should be followed as far as possible. Subjects that cannot be handled in this way should be played down, and referred to as little as possible.

If they do come up, or are brought up by the person to be motivated, a light touch—even humor, if feasible—is probably the best way to handle the situation. But this should definitely *not* be humor at the expense of the person to be motivated! It should relieve the situation, not emphasize it. Never let the other person believe that you are making fun of him or of something that is important to him!

How Good Handling of Disagreement Can Improve Your *Standing*

Of course it should be kept very much in mind that the quality of your *standing* often depends on the impression you give of having moral integrity, "good instincts," and strength of character. If the person to be motivated really values such qualities, he will be willing to recognize them and give credit for them, even when they appear as a result of a disagreement. In fact, a difference of opinion is usually the best opportunity to display independent judgment, original ideas, creative thinking, "the courage of your convictions," etc. People of intelligence usually respect someone who stands up for what he believes in.

How to Disagree and Stay Friends

The primary requirement in such situations would be to stick to your principles, but to be objective and reasonable; and above all, not to become emotional, or to let your "ego" become involved. Ending up with "that may be a better answer than this" can be lived with by both parties; but "*I*'m right and *you*'re wrong!" is hard to take, by anyone. Above all, *LISTEN* to the other person; give him the respect of paying attention to what he says, even if you *do* disagree.

Be constructive; be thoughtful; be sure you are at all times contributing helpfully, and not merely trying to "win." When others realize this, they will usually give you full credit for it. Such behavior is often appreciated and often admired. Mutual respect and even valuable friendships have resulted from honest disagreements honestly discussed, with mutual respect.

Avoid controversy as such; refrain from stubbornness; do not be contentious. Above all, do not allow disagreements to become personalized. If they must be faced, keep them on the basis of issues, not of personalities. That way, you can add to your *standing* by earning respect, not only for your ideas, but for the way you offer them. And so you can hope to motivate people, even when there is some disagreement between you.

3. HOW TO SLICE UP DISAGREEMENT TO FIND AREAS OF AGREEMENT

Earlier you saw how Johnny B. handled his disagreement with his boss. The boss thought Johnny was too young to be promoted. Johnny disagreed. Now, if Johnny had simply continued to disagree with his boss on that level, they would probably have come to a "You're too young!"—"No! I'm *not* too young!" confrontation. This kind of argument gets you nowhere. That would have been bad for both of them. And it would surely have stood in the way of Johnny motivating his boss to give him a promotion. In fact, it would probably have hurt Johnny's *standing*.

Johnny wisely avoided disagreement, and sought agreement, by slicing up the disagreement.

How Johnny B. "Sliced Up" His Disagreement with His Boss

"What does the boss really mean," Johnny asked himself, "when he tries to make *age* a condition for promotion? Surely it isn't only living a number of years that he has in mind. He must be thinking about the qualities that are associated with being on the job longer—being with the company longer. He must be thinking about experience, and the knowledge and know-how that you get on the job, and the reputation you can earn for reliability—things like that, that take some time.

"So," Johnny reasoned, "if I can just slice up our disagreement about age into a real consideration of the actual values that must be truly important to him, maybe we can come up with some agreement. Maybe I can get him to agree that I know enough, *now*; have had enough experience *already,* and am reliable enough to be promoted *now*. If so, maybe he'll promote me. And if not, at least I'll get a better reason why he won't, other than just that I'm too young. He'll have to give me a reason that I can work on —something I can get my teeth into—something that I can *do something* about!"

So Johnny went behind the disagreement on age, and looked for agreement on the issues that really counted. As soon as he could get his boss to agree that Johnny did have enough experience and knowledge to handle the promotion, and was reliable, the disagreement on age was side-tracked. Johnny was then well on the way to motivate his boss to consider him for the next vacancy upward.

How to Divide Disagreement to Find Some Agreement

Most opinions or attitudes are made up of many components; but people often think of them in an over-simplified way, and express themselves accordingly. Thus a disagreement may occur over the gross, combined expression, while there may be considerable agreement on many of the elements that enter into the two overall postures that seem to be in conflict.

Thus a Democrat and a Republican may disagree politically, but still agree on particular issues. A religious person and an atheist may agree on many virtues and values. An employee who likes his boss and another who dislikes the same boss can still agree on some of the boss' faults or qualities. And so it goes. There is almost always room for some agreement in any disagreement.

How to Look at a Point of View

A point of view, as usually held, is like what engineers call a *resultant* (of forces). It is something like the single force that results from the combined effects of a number of different (component) forces.

Think of it as being like a game of push-ball. In this game, two opposing teams are pushing on a huge ball. A number of players are each pushing for all they are worth, on all sides of the ball. So, of course, many different forces are working on the ball, all at once —in many different directions. There are many pushes, but only one ball; and it can only move in one direction at a time. Whichever way it moves, that direction is the *resultant*—the total effect—of all the different forces that are acting on the ball.

The forces exerted by the players on the same side are more-or-less in the same direction; the forces exerted by the players on the other side are more-or-less in the opposite direction. The forces in the same direction tend to reinforce one another; but the opposite forces tend to cancel each other out. The total effect of all the forces—the result of all the forces exerted on the ball in any direction—that total is the *resultant*; and that is the way the ball will move.

A person's point of view on any subject is really the *resultant* of many ideas, beliefs, feelings, needs, knowledge, experiences, attitudes, etc. that are all brought to bear, more or less, on a particular subject. There are the pros and the cons, and there are the "ifs" and the "maybes," and all sorts of other, more-or-less relevant factors that enter into his consciousness, or even remain in his subconscious. (Of course, some forces are much stronger than others).

As an example, if a public official is offered a really huge bribe, he may reject it forthwith as an insult to his integrity, or he may accept it as a way that some people use to get some things done for them. But he is far more likely to suffer some conflict. His honesty and loyalty, his sense of duty and decency, his conscience—will be supported by fear of exposure and fear of the consequent disgrace, punishment, effect on his family, etc. Working in the opposite direction will be his need for the money, and the temptation of all the things it might buy; and perhaps the belief that other officials are accepting bribes. His final decision will be deter-

1. *A and B disagree; their needs, interests, efforts and objectives are divergent*

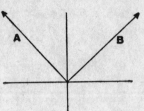

2. *A's direction is made up of two components: A₁ and A₂*

3. *B's direction is made up of two components: B₁ and B₂*

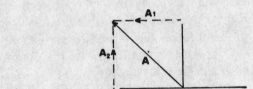

4. *A₁ and B₁ are opposed*

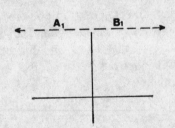

5. *But A₂ and B₂ are in exactly the same direction*

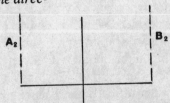

Finding a Common Interest

mined by the *resultant* of all such influences, working on his powers of decision.

The same principle applies to any motivation situation.

How You Can Find Some Agreement in Any Disagreement

Look at our diagram (Finding a Common Interest) which represents a serious disagreement between A and B. In 1 you see the two resultants, A and B, pointing in extremely divergent directions. This represents what seems to be a major—perhaps critical—area of disagreement between A, who wants to motivate B, and B. This could be Johnny B. and his boss disagreeing about Johnny being too young for promotion; or it could be Al T. and the Pinkhams disagreeing about the house being too large; or any other situation in which there is disagreement, and one person is trying to motivate another.

In #2 you see that A's resultant is really made up of two components: A_1 and A_2. (There are usually more components than this; but this will serve for illustration). In #3 you note that B's resultant is also really made up of two components: B_1 and B_2. Then in #4 we find that A's component A_1 and B's component B_1 are really diametrically opposed. This is the real area of disagreement.

But in #5 we find that A's component A_2 and B's component B_2 are both going in the same direction. This is an area of agreement!

Look for and find these areas of agreement, and make the most of them! They can help you to see how to slice up the disagreement, and emphasize the areas of agreement, so you can be more effective in motivating people. They can provide the *leverage* you need.

4. HOW AND WHEN TO MOTIVATE PEOPLE BY BEING FIRM

Firmness can have an important effect upon the motivations of others.

In some situations, of course, the person doing the motivating may be in a position to use insistence or threats as part of his motivational armory. For instance, if an employee is very strongly motivated to keep his job, he can be virtually forced into activity that is otherwise unacceptable to him, by the threat of losing it. In such cases, the motivation to keep his job is translated into the motivation to do as he is told to do; and this effect is then stronger than any opposing motivations—such as the motivation to avoid the task, to resist, to say "no!" to quit, etc. In such cases the boss has *standing* and *advantage* sufficient to operate a powerful *leverage* on the employee's strong motivation to keep his job.

How to Balance Motivations on Both Sides

But there are ways in which firmness can be used motivationally, even when the would-be motivator is not in the driver's seat. For instance, in motivating your boss, there is often a balancing of motivating effects on both sides. The boss desires to motivate you in a certain direction, and you let him know your own motivation —what it will take to motivate you. A kind of bargaining or negotiation takes place—frankly or indirectly—and so there is a trade-off of the two motivational leverages.

George F. was Manager of Warehousing and Distribution for a large chain store operation. He wanted to be given the title of vice-president; and this ambition was firmly held by him, and well known to his superiors. One day the Executive Vice-President of the company took him to lunch and told him that it was now regarded as desirable that he move his base from the company's head office in the East to a location in the Middle West. George really didn't want to make the move, and said so. He offered a series of well-thought-out objections, since he had already foreseen this development and was strongly motivated to resist it.

Finally the E.V.P. pulled out his trump card.

"We were going to put your name on the door of a nice, big office in Kansas City," he told George, "and we were going to put a mighty impressive title under it. Something like Vice-President, Warehousing and Distribution. How would *that* sound?"

It sounded pretty good to George. It was just what he had been wanting, for a long time. He had been persistent and persevering in his quest for such a title, and now his firmness had brought results. Management knew well of his long-held ambition; and they were using it at last, to motivate him to make a move they knew he wouldn't welcome on its own. This was a trade-off; a swap; an "I'll do this for you, if you'll do this for me" arrangement; an exchange of motivations. George's firmness had finally paid off; but the company got something for it.

How to Overcome Resistance to Change

When people are asked to do something they have not done before, to change from the familiar to the unfamiliar, they often resist. They have developed some degree of confidence and a sense of security in what they have been doing; and they have no such confidence and sense of security in what they are being asked to do. In such cases, adding incentives of higher pay, promotions or titles may motivate them; but such incentives do not really meet directly the negative motivations that arise from insecurity, uncertainty, and lack of confidence in one's ability to meet new standards, or to succeed in unfamiliar activities. Here there is need for motivational support of a different kind, and without that, receiving increased pay and higher status may simply add to the feeling of insecurity and of unfamiliarity, and thus increase the lack of confidence.

How Arthur B. Was Persuaded to Make a Big Switch

Arthur B. was a design engineer for a manufacturing company that produced special, often made-to-order equipment for use in certain industries. One day the plant superintendent sent for him. In the office he found both the Vice-President-Manufacturing, whom he knew as "the boss-of-the-boss of his boss"; and the Vice-President-Sales, whom he did not know.

The VP-M introduced the VP-S, and told Arthur: "Mr. Grant, here, wants you to be a salesman." Arthur was actually frightened—what was all this? Him—a salesman? He knew many of the salesmen—he often worked with them on special orders for customers. He was not like them!

The VP-S went into a lengthy pitch: he wanted Arthur not only to accept the transfer but to welcome it; he wanted to motivate Arthur to be pleased; to feel that the change was in his own best interests. Grant really wanted Arthur to be motivated to become a successful salesman. Arthur wasn't.

"But, Mr. Grant," Arthur protested, "I don't know anything about selling. I'm an engineer. My business is designing equipment. I'm a plant man—a drawing-board man. I'm no salesman."

"Wait a minute, now, Arthur," Grant replied. "Naturally, since you've never sold, you don't know that you can do it, and do it well. But *I* know that you can; and I know it because I know how

our equipment is sold, how our customers buy, and how our salesmen sell. And I know how you have helped a lot of our salesmen to
make sales. No peddling, no high-pressure, no talking anybody into
buying. Our customers have problems, and we solve them. They
need equipment—we make it. Nine-tenths of our selling is just
sitting down with a customer's engineers and learning exactly what
they need, so we can make it for them. You can do that as well as
anyone—it's right up your alley. Anything you need to know, we'll
teach you. I'll send you out with our best men—they'll soon show
you what's what. I *know* you can do it, and do it well."

Grant then went into the higher earnings and the greater prospects for promotion.

Finally the VP-M came back into the conversation.

"Arthur," he said, "I really believe this is in your own best
interest. If you stay in design engineering, your future is naturally
limited to your specialization. But as you learn other phases of our
business, you become available for more general responsibilities.
Of course, it does take some adjustment, some adaptation. Now, I'll
tell you what we'll do. You give it a try. I know it'll work out. But
promise me to give it at least three months. At the end of that time,
if you really want to get back to your old job, you come to me and I
promise it'll be waiting. But I'd like to see you make a go of *this*."

How Being Firm Can Help You to Motivate People

Arthur started out being strongly motivated *against* the new
job. But the others were firm with him, and they backed this firmness by helping Arthur to feel more confidence and security in the
new job; to see it in the context of familiar experience; to *perceive* it
as something he could handle. By building his sense of competence
to handle the new job, they enabled their firmness with him to bring
about enough motivation to try it. They persuaded him to test the
new job, and in so doing they were also testing him.

This kind of motivational effect is important. Motivation generally works toward changed behavior—often so greatly changed
that the individual to be motivated resists, because he fears and
wants to avoid change. In such cases effective reassurance, along
with firmness, becomes an essential part of the motivating process.
Once the individual develops some degree of confidence in his
ability to handle the change, the objections based on lack of confi-

dence disappear. Firmness thus can be necessary, with reassurance, to make the motivating process effective. Firmness holds the disagreement in check so the agreement can grow and build *advantage* to work on the *target motivation*.

5. HOW AND WHEN TO MOTIVATE PEOPLE BY YIELDING A POINT OR TWO

Too much firmness can motivate others in the wrong way. Rigidity may cause the wrong kind of relationship.

You cannot motivate someone else except as part of a relationship: the effect of motivation itself is a form of relationship. And, in any relationship, on either side, rigidity is likely to have undesirable effects. In highly organized situations subject to strict regulation and discipline, rigid relationships may be imposed, as in the military. But, as in the American military at least, such rigidity has been proven to be often self-defeating. The most effective commanders are seldom the most rigid.

In our culture, with the attitudes and social outlook that most Americans have, rigidity of relationship is often the enemy of motivation.

An Army officer who seeks to manage his men by rigid authority and discipline soon finds that he can rely, for motivation, only on his men's fear of the disciplinary consequences of failing to fulfill his wishes. He will have blocked, thrown away, killed off, any desire to please him, or any more constructive motivation; and with it, initiative, creativity, special effort, or any other contribution that he cannot demand and enforce.

How to Keep Rigidity and Authority from Working Against Your Purpose

In many individuals, the exercise of authority over them motivates a will to resist, to defy, to assert one's resentment—one's rejection of such treatment. Reactions like that, of course, make rigidity self-defeating, except among those who are willing to "live" with it; those, perhaps, who are accustomed to it through living in a culture or having a way of life that suggests the rigid, unquestioning discipline of Nazi organizations or of the Japanese Army of World War II.

To avoid rigidity is to invite mutual accommodation; and this requires yielding when appropriate. The boss who wants to motivate a subordinate to special effort had better be prepared to yield a point or two—if necessary, for instance, to meet that subordinate's request for scheduling an earned vacation. The subordinate who wants to motivate his boss to grant him a raise will do well to demonstrate his flexibility, for instance, about such matters as putting in extra time when necessary; and he will not be too rigid about running out at five o'clock every day.

How a "Give and Take" Attitude Can Help Your *Standing*

Graceful yielding lends a "give and take" quality to a relationship that can greatly improve an individual's *standing* with the other person. It can impart an atmosphere of reasonableness; of mutual accommodation; of constructive negotiation. It can involve a kind of bargaining or trade-off that brings mutual motivations into a mutually satisfactory arrangement, or deal. "You scratch my back; I'll scratch yours."

Jason S. had been a salesman, and a good one. But his wife became an invalid; and with three small children he felt that he could no longer spend so much time away from home, travelling. He had come to his boss, Irving L., the Sales Manager, with his problem, and Irving had agreed to make him Assistant Sales Manager for Administration—an office job.

Jason was just getting used to being at home evenings during the week, when a very effective salesman in the company's most important territory broke a leg, skiing. It was essential that his major accounts be taken care of; and Irving asked Jason to go back on the road, in that distant territory, until the injured salesman could return.

Jason had had a clear understanding with Irving that his new job would not require him to travel. And yet he understood clearly that Irving had a serious, unanticipated problem: it was quite important that the territory be covered, and there was no one else available to take care of it. Jason fully understood and sympathized with Irving's point of view; but he certainly didn't want to set a precedent whereby Irving would consider him as again generally available to travel. What to do?

Jason decided that he should yield; he owed it to Irving and to the company to take on the emergency assignment. His future with the company would be impaired if he refused, and he was strongly motivated to persevere, and develop that future. But at the same time he felt that his wife and children should not be the worse off for his travelling. So he went to Irving.

How Jason S. Motivated an Important Deal

"Irving," he began, "you know that I can't leave my wife and children without a competent person on hand. If I do go, I'll have to send for my wife's sister to stay in the house while I'm away; and I'll have to be back home every weekend. I want you to OK all expenses, including travel for my sister-in-law from Kankakee and return. I know you don't want me to be out of pocket on this. As soon as she gets here I'll be ready to go. OK?"

Jason had yielded gracefully to Irving. But he had also made it clear that he did not want to travel; and that acceptance of the assignment meant a real sacrifice. And this was emphasized by the way he involved Irving and the company in picking up the check for the cost of the essential arrangements. Jason was playing the part of the old reliable, the one who could always be counted on to come through, no matter what personal sacrifice—but who was not about to be taken advantage of!

By yielding in the way he did, he greatly added to his *standing*, and even built some *leverage*; and all this not only with his boss, but also with his boss's boss, the Vice-President-Marketing, to whom Irving reported: "I've been able to persuade Jason to handle the territory while Grogan is out. He didn't want to do it, of course, but he knew it had to be done, so he agreed. I guess we owe him for that."

How to Keep Your *Advantages* Strong

While graceful and appropriate yielding can build *standing*, and so help to motivate others, care must be taken not to yield when the effect may hurt the *motivation plan*. Such an adverse effect can come about through impairment of *advantages*, as a result of yielding on a vulnerable point.

This kind of self-defeating weakness is often observed in parents (and others) in some of the ways of dealing with their children. The child is indulged in the hope of motivating it to some desired pattern of behavior, but the result is that the child demands more indulgence, thus defeating the adult's original motivation. This could happen to Jason S., in the case cited above, if Irving L. began to make it a regular practice to ask him to undertake work that required travel. Sooner or later, Jason would be in the position of having to choose either to call a halt to travel, which might then jeopardize his job and would certainly hurt his *standing*; or agree to go on travelling, and thus defeat his own motivation in taking on what was to have been an office job, with no travelling.

Usually, in such situations, much more *standing* is lost by refusing to yield, *after* having yielded on a previous occasion, than by refusing to yield in the first place. If a person yields once, the other party has a far greater reason for expecting him to yield again, than he had for expecting him to yield in the beginning.

It is better to be firm at the start—as firmness is discussed in the previous section—than to yield (however gracefully) if yielding is likely to place you at a strategic disadvantage by subjecting you to further pressure to yield when you will be extremely reluctant to do so, and when you may even feel compelled to resist. Try not to let yielding become a precedent.

When Yielding Is a Pleasure

And then, of course, there is the kind of yielding that brings real satisfaction—when you graciously consent to do what you always wanted to do all along!

Remember Tom Sawyer, who got his friends to whitewash his Aunt's fence by "yielding" to their pleas (and payments) to be allowed to do what he wanted them to do? *That* had a great motivational effect, while it would have been futile for him to ask them to do it for him. However, don't be too triumphant, or those who have been motivated to the *target behavior* you planned for, may have a negative reaction—then your *advantage* may not be so effective, next time.

8

DEVELOPING A
SYSTEMATIC ABILITY TO
APPLY MOTIVATIONAL LEVERAGE

As you learn more and more about utilizing Motivational Leverage, you will develop a greater understanding of where and how to apply it, and you will begin to use it on a day-to-day basis, almost without having to think about it specifically—almost automatically. Of course, in the more important situations, you will want to make a much greater effort. This chapter offers suggestions about thinking ahead and considering the future; and also about working out the most effective strategies, and applying the right Motivational Leverage techniques to make them succeed.

1. HOW TO MULTIPLY YOUR FUTURE "POTENTIALS"

When you find that you need to motivate people, it is very helpful if they are already favorably disposed toward you. In many cases, that *standing* may be all you need.

There is an old saying that tells us "You can never have too many friends.'' This is really just another way of saying that you can always benefit by having others already motivated or ready to be motivated in your favor.

This can be true upward or downward. ''Those in high places,'' or even those with a small seniority or one step of authority over you can often offer or withhold or influence an opportunity, soften or make more harsh the effects of an adverse development, and render pleasant or unpleasant an assignment or any other experience.

And we never know when someone below us in status or in a normal relationship can play a vital role in our lives; or at least make a substantial difference in some situation of importance to us. In Aesop's famous fable, the mouse promised that if the lion would spare him, some day he would repay the favor. The lion laughed, but let him go. Later the mouse found the lion helpless, caught in a net; and the mouse saved the lion's life by gnawing through the cords.

Recognizing the Importance and Value of Good Will

Subordinates, of course, have it in their power to ''make or break'' a superior; they can make him appear incompetent, or they can make him look good. And anyone who sells knows only too well the importance of the goodwill of customers.

In truth, we cannot afford to miss the possibilities of causing people to be motivated favorably toward us, whether we are dealing with a boss, a relative, a subordinate, a customer, a business contact, an associate, a neighbor, a social acquaintance, or, indeed, with anyone else.

The possibilities are endless; and the careers of successful people are marked by the indispensable contributions of others to their successes. Examples range from the favorably disposed ''big shot,'' who can ''open the door'' for you, down to the stenographer who corrects the grammar of dictated letters or the office boy who calls attention to a disorder in appearance; from the first supervisor who instills a sense of ''how to get along,'' to the Board Chairman who controls high-level careers; from the friendly, helpful youth at the next desk, to the labor union official who allows a way for management and employees to ''live together''; etc.

The possibilities for benefiting through the initiative, facilitation, patronage, intercession, or even the mere friendly guidance or informative word of others are virtually unlimited. Any limits are set only by the number and scope of contacts, the potential contribution (of any kind) by those contracts, and the disposition of those contracts to make such contributions when they might count.

How Others' Attitudes Toward You Can Have Long-Term Effects

Perhaps we are never free of this kind of dependence upon others. Even many of those who have "climbed to the heights" have found their own past to be suddenly a subject of wider interest to others. And then the attitudes of former associates may once again be brought into focus, so motivations of the past again have the opportunity to influence the present. The way former associates felt about you long ago may have an effect upon your future, tomorrow.

Simon D. and Allen J. both had successful careers in the accounting department of a very large retail chain. When the Controller died suddenly of a heart attack, they both came under consideration for the post. The Vice-President of Finance instituted a rather thorough check into both candidates' past records, including interviews with those who had worked closely with them at all stages of their careers.

And so the opportunity came to Anthony L., now the supervisor of the Accounts Payable Section, to act upon his long-standing motivations toward Simon D. and Allen J.

"Simon's okay," Anthony told the Vice-President of Finance, "but Allen has a terrible temper. His face gets red as a brick, and he can hardly talk. Maybe he has learned how to control it. But oh, boy! If he hasn't, some people better watch out!"

Anthony had worked under both Simon and Allen quite a few years before, when each was new in his first supervisory position. Anthony had "tested the limits" with them, and Simon had handled it well; but Allen, not yet secure in his new job, had reacted violently. Allen's *standing* with Anthony, from long ago, was thus strongly negative; and this liability lay dormant for all those years until at last it found the chance to express itself. Allen's career was temporarily derailed, as a result, while Simon received helpful support to an important promotion.

The Enduring Value of Positive *Standing*

Negative *standing* can be like a piece of unexploded ordnance left lying around after a war—like a land mine or a "dud" bomb. There is no telling when it may go off, or what damage it may do, unless it is defused or disposed of.

Some executives understand this principle very well, and are at pains to be rid of possible "enemies." In one well-known case, the post of chief executive officer of a major corporation became open. Three senior vice-presidents competed for it, but the directors finally chose an "outsider"—they brought in a top executive of another company. Almost the first act of the new Chief Executive Officer was to get rid of his three rivals and competitors. He was taking no chances on their hostile motivations.

It is difficult, if not impossible, to avoid oppositional situations with others entirely, especially if one is active, displays initiative, and stands up for one's own opinions. But such worthwhile characteristics need not result in negative *standing*—need not arouse the adverse motivations of others. The saving factor involves keeping all issues on the objective level of principle, and avoiding personalities. It is essential to avoid letting personalities be tied to issues, or the whole situation becomes distorted into conflict over "Who wins?" rather than "What is best?"

How to Avoid Negative *Standing*

The higher levels of major corporations are studded with forceful, determined individuals who have left behind them many subdued or defeated colleagues; whose adverse motivations, though not sufficient to block their advances, may have slowed these or made them difficult. But there are also those who, despite their successful dynamism, appear to have no enemies; and who, indeed, enjoy the sincere support, admiration and affection of most of those with whom they have been in contact.

They did not win such favorable motivation of others by not competing, by refraining from all controversy, by taking no stands, or by making the avoidance of conflict a primary goal. Rather, they won it by consistently showing fairness and a strong dedication to unselfish objectives and impersonal principles. Anyone who is offended by such conduct probably has only himself to blame, and will win little sympathy from others.

Sincere pursuit of logical goals for the general benefit of the organization or group divorces the behavior from the taint of self-interest, while still offering the fullest scope for ability, judgment, skill, personality, etc. It is least likely to invoke adverse motivations; and most likely to bring about the respect and the long-term, favorable motivations of others. In this way it can both multiply and maximize the opportunities—often unforeseen, and far in the unpredictable future—for ultimately benefiting through having motivated others favorably and through having gained favorable *standing* with them, even without having made this a specific objective. Those who learn how to do this usually find they have many friends when they need them. Then it is not only a matter of "yea, I used to know the——!" but rather, "He was O.K!"

2. HOW TO CHOOSE YOUR MOST ADVANTAGEOUS COURSE

In a previous section we discussed generalized possibilities and how to multiply them through the fostering of favorable *standing*. The more possibilities we have, of course, the greater choice we have as to the ones we may wish to follow or exploit.

Some people, however, make the mistake of trying to "keep all options open." It would be wonderful, of course, if we could take advantage of *all* possibilities; but this is manifestly impractical. However, it is always a matter of regret when we give up any possibility. As a result, we seldom do this consciously or deliberately; we seldom face the fact that, when we make a choice, we may be closing the door to another possibility that holds some attractions.

What happens is that we often allow possibilities to escape us—to fade away or die—through neglect. When we cannot follow up *all* attractive possibilities, we select some and give them most or all of our time and attention. The other possibilities then go to others or fade away.

What to Do About Good Possibilities You Cannot Use Now

The important consideration here is that we should not unnecessarily and carelessly ignore or reject the helpful motivations of others toward us. If someone offers to help you, for instance, toward Objective B, and you have selected Objective A, what should you do about it?

Sally D. was in her sixth year with the Capitol Foods Company, and she had been doing well. Two years ago she was promoted from a job in Market Research to be an Assistant Section Manager in Distributor Relations. Her old boss, under whom she had served in Market Research, was Chad B. He came to her one day and suggested that she return to Market Research as a Junior Project Manager—a nice step upward. But her present Section Manager, Ed C., had indicated that she might replace him whenever he moved up, as expected, and became Assistant Department Head of Distributor Relations. That would give Sally an even bigger step up, at some later time.

Sally naturally preferred the bigger promotion, so she assured Ed that she wanted to take advantage of the possibility he offered. At the same time, she knew that the realization of this development was not entirely certain, and in any case was some time off. So she did not discourage Chad. In fact, she indicated interest in his suggestion, in order to keep that possibility open.

What Happened to Chad B.'s Good Will

So Chad went to bat for her one day, when the opening for Junior Project Manager came up in Market Research; and the decision was made to offer her the job. But in the meantime matters had been moving ahead in Distributor Relations: Ed had been privately assured of his own promotion, to take place at the beginning of the next year; he had nominated Sally to take his place, and the nomination had been favorably received at the upper levels.

Therefore, when the offer of the position of Junior Project Manager was formally made to Sally, she had to take it or leave it. She could no longer postpone, delay, procrastinate, or try to keep both possibilities open indefinitely. She had to decide; so she turned it down. And so, of course, that was the last time Chad—or anyone else in Market Research—ever went to bat for her.

Chad had felt fully authorized to bespeak the job for her; he had done so wholeheartedly; and now she had rejected it. He was put in an embarrassing position, and all because "she had let him down." Her *standing* with him became negative; her *advantage* disappeared. Chad's favorable motivation toward her was turned into resentment and distrust—into adverse motivation.

Sally later gained a fine promotion, but she lost a friend—and she did this quite unnecessarily. By refraining from telling Chad what he had a right to know, she had allowed him to go ahead on her behalf. He had done so for her; and then she had "jerked the rug out from under him"—at least, that was how it looked to Chad. She "bit the hand that fed her," "climbed and kicked the ladder away," "burnt the bridges behind her," etc.

What You Can Learn from Sally D.'s Experience

Sally should—at least—have kept Chad informed. If she had told him of the situation in Distributor Relations, he would have understood that the possibility there was naturally preferable to her. Quite possibly he would still have nominated her for the Junior Project Manager position, on the off-chance that it might work out. But he would have avoided putting himself in the false position of assuring his seniors that Sally wanted that position.

There's an old fable of Aesop's about the dog carrying a bone across a brook, and catching sight of his own reflection in the water below. Eager to take the bone away from the dog he saw there, he dropped the bone he carried and snatched at the reflection. Thus, in his eagerness to have two bones, he lost the one he had.

Sally's performance was not quite so tragic, but she did lose something of value—something that might prove quite important at some later date.

How to Redirect Others' Helpfulness Toward the Goals You Choose

It is important, very often, to make a clear, deliberate choice between or among the possibilities; and then to concentrate on the possibility chosen. When such a choice is made, it is important to consider carefully what must be given up. Very often a possibility may be abandoned *without* losing all the possible advantages related to it.

The favorable motivations of others can often be redirected to a different objective. For instance, if Sally had told Chad she wanted to concentrate on getting the job of Section Manager in Distributor Relations, he probably could and would have found ways to help her.

When you are making a choice between alternative directions, there are probably many factors to be considered. Among these some of the most important—perhaps the critical ones—may be the motivations of others. This may be the time to test your *standing,* your *advantages,* with those who may make or influence the decisions that will determine your success or failure in achieving the objective you are choosing.

At such a time you should give serious consideration to the frankest discussion with the appropriate individuals, about the situation, the problem you face, and the variables—as you see them. Many times such a discussion has brought about—or brought to light—invaluable information about the relevant attitudes and motivations of principals in the matter; or, at least, information and advice not previously available, derived from superior understanding of the situation (as recommended especially in Chapter 6).

Be Sure You Know the Score

Arnold G., a researcher with a small brokerage firm, was concerned about his future. He was seriously thinking of quitting—looking for a job elsewhere, or taking courses at night to prepare himself for a better job. He decided to ask for an appointment with the partner who had general supervision over the personnel of the firm—a man he scarcely knew.

During the interview he spoke quite frankly of his doubts about his future with the firm, his own ambitions and the options he had considered. He requested an equally frank reaction.

He then learned for the first time that the firm was about to enlarge, taking in several new partners; and would expand its research capabilities. The partner indicated that Arnold was in line for promotion to manager of a section in the enlarged department. So Arnold decided to begin his courses, and to wait and see what would happen at the office. He decided it was the wrong time to quit.

Arnold was able to choose the direction he wanted to go on the basis of the fullest available knowledge and understanding of the possibilities and significant factors that could be available to him, which he had gained through his own frankness. And he built some *standing* for himself as he did this; and it worked out well for him.

3. HOW TO PICK A WINNING STRATEGY

Unless you hope or expect to arrive at some happy state by

accident, you should take some steps to make up your mind as to: 1) what you really want to have happen; 2) how much of that you can make happen; and 3) how to go about making it happen. Only then, really, can you do something about it intelligently, to make it more likely that you will get to where you want to go. Have a purpose; and have a plan; and be realistic about what to do and how to do it.

To succeed in your purpose, you will almsot certainly need some help, encouragement, support, backing, or other favorable disposition or action by or from others. First, you should know or find out who these people are (*target individuals*). Then you should know or find out just what attitudes or actions on their part are necessary for your purpose (*target behavior*). And after that you can begin to work out how to motivate them, as necessary, to have them do as you want them to do (*motivation plan*). (This is discussed in Chapter 6.)

The Basic Key to Effective *Leverage*

If you are to succeed by any means other than by luck, you will have to be realistic. You will have to have a purpose that you can reasonably expect to attain. There is no great harm in dreaming; but if you try to act on a dream you are probably being foolish.

Of course, there are people of great vision who see possibilities that others do not see, and surprise all those who "knew them when" by the wonderful successes they achieve. But their dreams turn out to have been realistic, and not only dreams, after all.

There are a few strong individuals, with great faith in themselves, who somehow *know* they can accomplish far more and rise much higher than even their families and friends expect of them. But there are far more unrealistic hopefuls who are only fooling themselves; whose notions of their own abilities or of the value of their ideas are not reflected in the cold objectivity of the outside world. A very few of these, who may really be geniuses, may ultimately be proven right; but then we are talking about rare exceptions. Most of us have to live with the realities of the work-a-day world and its values.

Making People Believe Your Objectives Are Realistic

The point here is that, when it comes to motivating people to help you reach your target, *they* have to have some belief in the realism of *your* purpose. If they do not believe that your hopes or expectations are reasonable, their motivations will be hung up on an impossible obstacle. If they think you are aiming too high, or that too many others with better chances are aiming at the same competitive goal, they will figure your chances are too small to justify their trying to help.

A youngster just out of college, working as a trainee under a department head, can probably motivate his boss to help him win promotion as a first-level supervisor—after he has shown the ability and the attitudes that qualify him for the position. But if he asks for a quick jump upward of several levels, his boss will only question his good judgment.

Other people have their own "picture" of you; and it bears some relation to their own pictures of themselves. Your own picture of yourself may be quite different, but they can only be motivated in relation to *their* picture of you—and you may have to change this before you have the *standing* you need to motivate them as you wish.

Charlie H. was an ambitious young go-ahead specialist in market research. He was promoted from being a junior supervisor in the Market Research Section of a large consumer goods company to be assistant to a Product Manager, Will D. Will liked Charlie; and he was soon motivated to help Charlie develop himself to qualify for a Product Manager spot.

Charlie was wise enough to realize that Will had been looking at him only as a promising junior. He would not welcome the idea that Charlie might someday be over him, perhaps even far above him, as vice-president of marketing. In fact, Will would probably resent that Charlie was even thinking of himself in terms of such great achievement—far greater than Will had ever imagined for himself. So Charlie kept his greater ambition to himself, and concentrated on the next step. On this step he had Will motivated to help him; and so he made the grade.

A few years later, when he had shown not only his ability to handle the new position, but also his potential to go even higher, Charlie attracted the favorable attention of executives on higher levels. And then, when some of them asked Will about Charlie, Will was pleased to give him a boost. He had become adjusted to the realization that Charlie was going to rise past him; his perspective had developed. Will even had a certain pride in having "launched"

Charlie, and now accepted the idea that Charlie was on the way up. He could even get some satisfaction out of the fact that "he knew him when."

How to Help People Adust to and Accept Your Objectives

Charlie had correctly estimated not only his own potential, but also the problems and possibilities of motivating Will to support him. He had always had a definite picture of his own ambition; but he "kept his eye on the ball," and so he was able to motivate Will to support him when he needed it, as he could not have done if he had talked about his ultimate goal at the beginning—much too soon.

It is all very well to "aim at the stars," providing you *can* and *do* get as far as "the backyard fence." An idea that looks into the future may be a dream or a plan; but a plan, even when keeping one eye on the same summit as that of the dream, also keeps an eye on the first step.

"The longest voyage begins with a single step," and to do anything in a purposive, rational way you must see both the ultimate objective and the immediate objective—the goal, and the nearest sub-goal. And, since making each step may need the support of others, it is vital to think in terms of motivating others for each step.

Building Step-by-Step Toward Your Long-Term Goals

Only the fortunate few find anyone outside their families who is or can be really motivated to help them reach remote, long-term, far-off goals; and who is also in a position to help them. Most of the time, it is only practical to concentrate on motivating people for limited and specific purposes—purposes that are realistic, and that also seem to them desirable for you (and usually are also in some way, favorable for them). People can be difficult to motivate, even for desirable goals, especially if those goals seem to them too far off, or too difficult to attain.

Remember the story of the little boy who came home one afternoon and said, "I almost got a white horse today"? His mother asked him what he meant, and he answered, "I saw a man with a nice white horse. I asked him if I could have it, and he said no. If he had said yes, I would have a white horse."

Of course, the little boy's goal was quite unrealistic; and the man had no motivation to help him achieve it. If the boy had asked to pat the horse, or even to sit on it, the man might well have been motivated to let him do it. (Handled cleverly, the episode might have resulted in the boy persuading his family to buy him a pony.)

Set up your real, realistic objective; then outline the steps you need to take, and realistically believe you can take, that should lead to the attainment of that objective. That is the strategy, and a major part of developing your strategy consists of thinking through— realistically—whom you need to motivate, and how you will motivate them. But always remember that this is always most important for the *next* step. That calls for tactics, which we consider in the next section.

4. HOW TO DEVELOP YOUR TACTICS TO MAKE YOUR STRATEGY SUCCEED

When you begin to put your plan into effect, you will need to work out detailed planning for each sub-goal—each step or stage of the overall plan. This kind of activity, with immediate or very-close-up results, involves tactics.

The classical parallel comes from the military, with Headquarters working out the overall strategy of the campaign, and assigning objectives (tactical objectives) to the field commands, which then work out their own tactics to carry out these immediate objectives against the enemy.

In the same way, you should have your overall plan for reaching your own ultimate goal; and then you should work out the detailed plan for each phase of the overall plan, as you move from one phase to the next. *Motivation plans* for different *target individuals* along the way are part of the planning; and you carry them out as tactics.

How Bert N. Planned His Tactics to Support His Motivation Strategy

Bert N. did a good job of planning his strategy and developing his tactics when he sold to a major food manufacturer a big contract for advertising space in the publication he represented. He began in January with an overall strategic plan that he hoped would get him a contract for the next year. He would gather all the information and work out all the arguments and be prepared to emphasize all the benefits; and he would use the appropriate elements of all this, tactically, with each individual who could influence the decision;

and he would develop a special *motivation plan* to fit each one of these.

He began with the advertising agency that handled the account. First he had several sessions with the media buyer, in which he made sure that the man had all the technical information on circulation, readership, rates and so forth that he would need to come to a favorable attitude. Then he saw the account executive, and got him interested; and he followed up with the copywriter and the art director. After that he went to the food company's advertising manager, and sold him on the advantages. He went on, through product managers and sales manager up to the marketing vice-president; and with each one he followed different tactics that were appropriate for their special interests and responsibilities; and that were also adapted to their personalities, and responsive to their attitudes.

The result was that he got a lot of people interested and favorably inclined; so much so that he was able to arrange a special presentation, in the food company's board room. The company president and the agency president sat in, along with all the others that Bert had already motivated. And so it was no accident that the company's advertising budget carried a substantial sum to buy the space that Bert had been aiming to sell. Bert's strategic plan worked; and it worked because he planned sound tactics to make it work; and his tactics were successful because he picked all the right *targets*, and he carried out effective *motivation plans* with each of them. Bert's commission was a large one, and he had earned it.

Planning a Successful Long-Term Strategy

Madeleine G. rose all the way from salesgirl to Vice-President of Merchandising in a large woman's wear retail chain by working out a sound strategic plan, and then planning the appropriate tactics, and carrying them out successfully. She laid out a practical plan of progression from one position to another, leading upward toward the top.

Her first boss was a woman who was Section Head over lingerie in the store where Madeleine began. She had come up the hard way, slowly, by putting in long hours; and by showing herself, over the years, to be dutiful and reliable and very hardworking. Madeleine saw that she would have to show herself to be similarly dedicated and hardworking if she was to make a favorable impression on this woman; and so she laid out her tactics accordingly. She really worked hard. Her *motivation plan* succeeded with this *target*, and she was moved up to fill the next vacancy, as Section Head, herself, in another of the company's stores.

Her next boss, the store manager, was a man who had studied retailing in college and believed in "working smart" rather than laboriously. So Madeleine changed her tactics accordingly: she enrolled in evening courses in retail management, fashion and merchandising; and her tactics now included a *motivation plan* aimed at this very different *target*. She showed herself clever, adaptable, and quick to learn.

In accordance with her strategic planning, her new tactics succeeded; she motivated her second boss to recommend her to fill a vacancy as assistant lingerie buyer in the head office of the chain. There her boss was a very clever business woman who, as a *target*, required still a different *motivation plan*; and so Madeleine developed a new set of tactics to fit the new situation.

And so it went; the general plan had to be changed somewhat, a few times, but for the most part her strategy stood up very well; and it was successful because she carried it out, step-by-step, with the right tactics for each sub-goal. And that is how she rose to be Vice-President of Merchandising for the retail chain.

Developing Your Tactics to Produce the Specific Results You Want

In developing your tactics, you must have clearly in mind the results you want to achieve. You must consider, on the one hand, how these results can be brought about; and, on the other hand, what you can do to bring them about. In between, you consider what other people can do to bring about or help to bring about those results. From this, you pick your *targets* and set up your *motivation plans* for them, and then determine the best way that is open to you, to carry out your *motivation plans* and also to do whatever else you need to do and can do to produce the results you are after. From this you develop your tactics—what you will do, and how you will do it.

Of course, it is always possible that something in the situation will change. Some additional element may enter; a new personality may appear; an event may introduce new factors. Relationships change; attitudes alter. Be alert to how such changes may affect the appropriateness of your tactics; and be ready to adapt your tactics to the changed situation.

How to Be Sure You Are on the Right Track, by Checking As You Go Along

Even without any significant changes in the situation, it is very important, as you go along, to ask yourself how you are doing; and to check as carefully and fully and accurately as you can to see how your tactics are working. You may need to modify or improve them. Be honest with yourself about this. Be objective; do not let yourself be deceived by false optimism, nor discouraged by unjustified pessimism. But you should never assume that your tactics are the best you can use. It is often advantageous to modify them in some way, even when they appear to be working.

Here is a checklist for you to keep in mind:

Your strategy must be related to your prime (long-term) goal.
Your general plan must be related to your strategy.
Your general plan should include logical sub-goals.
Your tactics must be adapted to and designed to achieve each sub-goal.
Your tactics must provide for motivating those whose help or goodwill you need.
Your tactics must include a *motivation plan* for each *target*.

From time to time, check your strategy, your general plan and your tactics against this checklist to make sure you are being realistic—that they really fit the circumstances and conditions under which they must work for you.

5. HOW TO APPLY TECHNIQUES THAT FIT YOUR TACTICS

In every activity there is the element of technique. You can pick the right targets, make excellent plans, even design excellent tactics—and still fail in reaching your goal because of something left out, or something extra put in, or something not done in the right way, so that what you do just does not fit the situation or the target.

It is something like a very musical person trying to learn to play an unfamiliar instrument—the violin, for instance. He may know and have great feeling for the music, and understand the instrument perfectly in theory; but unless he fingers the strings and handles the bow with appropriate technique, he cannot sound right.

The most dangerous errors of technique, of course, result in motivating people differently than, or even contrary or opposite to the direction you want. Sometimes these poor results seem like resistance; sometimes like stubbornness; and sometimes just like plain, old-fashioned contrariness, or even meanness. But there is always a reason; and if you can figure it out, you should be able to do something about it.

Using the Right Techniques to Make Your Tactics Work

The most common error of technique often occurs when you let someone know that you intend to motivate him. There is a big difference between telling someone you have a goal, and telling someone you are depending on them to help you reach it. There is an even bigger difference between getting someone to think it is their own idea to do as you wish, and forcing them to realize that if they do it, it is only because you are working to get them to do it. One way, they feel they are "being noble"; the other way, they feel they are being "used."

Letting People Think that Helping You Is *Their* Idea

In general, people tend to like the idea that they do things because *they* want to do them; because *they* think it is best; and not just because someone else is trying to get them to do it, or making it difficult for them not to do it. This principle applies even in the most intimate relationships: a husband likes to feel that he is giving or doing out of the goodness of his heart, out of his love and generosity—because he wants to—and not because he is talked into it or cajoled or even nagged into it by his wife. A parent likes to feel that he or she indulges a child of their own free will, and not out of impatience with the child's endless importunity. When they see a person they have tried to help improve or get ahead in any way, they like to take the credit—or some of it—for themselves. They may be very resentful of having someone else claim it—even the person himself.

It is perfectly true that persistent reminder and repeated demand can sometimes wear down resistance and bring about change. But in most instances, probably, the same result might very well have come about without all that wearing down. The employee who keeps on demanding a raise or a promotion may finally get it; but probably not before or not much before he would have got it anyhow, since raises and promotions are not often knowingly given when undeserved, unless the demand leaves no acceptable alternative.

Why Working from the Inside Is Better than Working from the Outside

It is perhaps difficult to appreciate the difference between the kind of motivational activity that is truly and constructively effective, and the kind that seeks almost to force a change of behavior in the desired direction. The first works from *inside* the person being motivated; the other attempts to impose motivation from the outside. The first relies on *standing* and *advantage* to provide the necessary *leverage;* the second tries to apply *leverage* at a sacrifice of *standing* and *advantage*.

How Gil S. Motivated "From the Inside"

Gil S. was a District Manager of Sales for a pharmaceutical firm; he supervised ten of the "detail men" who called on doctors to promote the company's products. One of his men, Art K., was outstanding in almost every way. He knew the company's products thoroughly; he knew the competitive products; he understood very well the medical considerations, the pharmacology and the biochemistry of the treatments involved; and he was hard-working, and skilled in scheduling his calls. There was only one major drawback: Art tended to be too positive. He was too aggressive when he was talking to the doctors—almost arrogant. He expounded his sales arguments so strongly that many doctors resented it. His "hard sell" often "put their backs up."

Gil made up his mind he was going to get Art to change this bad habit: he would motivate Gil to cut down on his forcefulness, and so make his presentations more acceptable to the doctors.

Gil himself had worked for several years under a District Manager who had treated him very much as Art treated the doctors: he used to say what he had to say forcefully, assertively, commandingly, often bruising the listener's sensitivities. Gil remembered how he had resented the absolute criticism and the uncompromising direction. It was as if the man said, "I know, and you don't. So you'd better listen to me, and do as I say; only then may you be able to do it well." Gil resolved not to try to motivate Art in this way.

Gil spent a couple of days, every month, accompanying Art on his calls. He brought along a small, portable tape recorder; and he recorded many of the interviews, inconspicuously. When he had a number of such interviews taped, he went over them and picked out half a dozen in which Art's pitches had been most aggressive, and the doctors' responses showed most clearly their unfavorable reactions.

One late afternoon, after a long day of calls, Gil played these interviews back to Art. Gil made no comment at first. He only said, "Art, I want you to listen to these six interviews, and tell me what you think."

Art listened. His face got a little red, and he didn't say anything for a while. Finally he asked: "Gil—do you think maybe I push them a little too hard?" He had certainly got the message.

"It isn't what *I* think," Gil answered. "It's what the doctors think." Art really got the point; and he asked Gil to help him moderate the tone of his detailing.

Influencing Others Without Provoking Resistance

If Gil had simply told Art that his pitches were alienating the doctors, Art would not have believed him; and he would have resisted the idea of changing. But, instead, Gil had helped him to see clearly, for himself, what was wrong and what needed to be done.

Some people, of course, are eager for constructive criticism, and for help in improving themselves. This is most likely to be true when they are not expected to be "perfect"—like younger people or new employees, or those on new routines, and so their egos are not too closely bound up with the activities in question. With such employees, constructive criticism and helpful guidance can, in themselves, be highly and effectively motivating.

But many others are not ready or willing or glad to accept criticism, or direction in changing their ways of doing things. And they will be difficult to motivate until they accept the idea of the desirability of change. Very often this has to be suggested to them in a way that does not arouse defensive resistance—that does not offend their pride or violate their image of themselves. (See Section 2 in this chapter.)

When you select your *target individual,* make sure you know what kind of technique to use.

9

HOW TO USE MOTIVATIONAL LEVERAGE EVEN IN THE MOST DIFFICULT SITUATIONS

Some situations involving other people can be extremely difficult. People misunderstand one another, and persist in such misunderstandings. People allow pride to interfere with reason. Insecurity makes some people act unreasonably. Some people have troublesome "angles." And some disagreements are so bitter they seem hopeless. This chapter suggests how Motivational Leverage may be useful, even in such difficult situations as these.

1. HOW YOU CAN RESOLVE MISUNDERSTANDING

Whatever it is that you want someone else to do, it has a certain value for you, and a certain value for them. If the values are positive for both of you—that is, if what you want them to do is also agreeable, pleasant, desirable or acceptable to them—then motivating them should not be difficult. In fact, the basis for the motivation already exists. However, if what you want them to do is disagreeable, unpleasant, undesirable or unacceptable to them, then, of course, the motivation is very likely to be quite difficult.

But there is still another, rather common kind of motivational situation, in which there is some degree of misunderstanding. In such situations, typically, people may believe that what you want them to do is less agreeable, pleasant, desirable or acceptable than you say it is, or than you believe it to be. In fact, they may believe that what you want them to do is downright disagreeable, unpleasant, undesirable or unacceptable, even when you are sure it is not, or should not be, to them.

There are, of course, all kinds of examples of this sort of situation. These can range from persuading someone to eat something that is new and—to them—dubious, to getting someone to take on a job he is not sure he can handle, or will like, as in the case of George F. (See Chapter 7, Section 4.)

How Differences in Past Experience Can Cause Disagreement

There are two major kinds of factors or influences that operate in such cases, to cause misunderstanding. These are related. They are experience, and personal tastes or values. If you have learned to swim, jumping into the water is no problem to you. But the simple prospect of jumping into the water may terrify someone who has never done it, and who cannot swim. The difference here is entirely in the individual's own past; and the difference is so great that you would find it difficult to motivate the fearing one merely by pointing out that *you* are not afraid! And, if you press the matter, your attitude may be seriously resented as harsh, cruel, aggressive, bullying, etc.—when you only meant to be friendly, encouraging, helpful, reassuring, etc. Of course, it is difficult to motivate someone to do something which is strange and new to them, and which may also seem to be dangerous.

Also, there is the difference in taste, or values—really another kind of difference in experience. Suppose that you are travelling in a strange city with another person, and they want to go to an art gallery, and you want to take in a prize fight. There is probably a basic difference in tastes between you. If either one is able to persuade the other, the persuaded one will probably have to be motivated by something other than the motivation that is acting upon his persuader. For instance, if the one who isn't interested in art ends up by going along to view the paintings and sculpture, it will probably be because he is motivated by not wanting to be left alone, or not wanting the other person to be alone, or some other consideration, rather than because he has been converted to a strong motivation to see the art.

How Your *Standing* Can Support What You Say, to Influence People

When you are trying to motivate or persuade someone, it should be useful to remember that the other person will be affected by the way he "sees" (perceives) you—as having an outlook on life that is rather similar to or rather different from his own. If someone knows that you like the same things and are usually in agreement with him about most matters that come up, he will have some confidence in your views, tastes, attitudes or opinions. This is an important kind of *standing*.

But substantial differences in age, experience, wealth, occupation, lifestyle, taste or other personal matters will work against understanding, or even against willingness to accept what is said. The person who likes to eat plain, simple, bland cooking, and who knows that you like exotic, or highly seasoned, complex, gourmet dishes will simply not be convinced by your assurance that the *hasenpfeffer* or the goat-meat curry is delicious. He knows that "delicious" to you is not the same as "delicious" to him.

How to Use a Third Party to Make Someone See Things Your Way

If you really want such a person to try something exotic, then the thing to do is to get someone to recommend it whom that person knows really likes corned beef and cabbage, hamburgers or spaghetti. That "third person" will have the right *standing* to be convincing about that subject.

The technique advised here is almost like using an interpreter when two people do not speak the same language. A third party, who speaks both languages, can help them to understand one another.

Doris F., supervisor of a clerical section in an insurance company, wanted to move young Natalie N. up to an operation rather more complicated than the one she had been handling. But Natalie was extremely hesitant to make this move. She lacked confidence; and she was quite unconvinced by Doris' assurances that she would soon learn to perform the new operation easily and in a relaxed way.

Doris was a college graduate, a supervisor, smartly dressed, and obviously on the way up. But Natalie was of a poor, relatively uneducated, immigrant background. She lacked confidence in herself; and she felt herself to be so different, so "apart" from Doris, that a statement by Doris that "this new job is easy" had no real motivating effect for her. It only meant that the new job would be easy for Doris! So she resisted being switched—advanced—to the new work. She really misunderstood the situation; and was even suspicious that Doris was trying to force her into a situation she could not handle.

Fortunately, there was another girl in the section with a background similar to Natalie's, and she had been working successfully on the new procedure for some time. This was Maria Lopez; and Doris finally thought of asking her to help persuade Natalie.

And Maria had little trouble doing this. Natalie easily identified with Maria—this was someone very much like herself. If Maria could do it, then she, Natalie, could also learn to do it. So Natalie was easily persuaded, motivated, by a third person—Maria—to do what Doris, by herself, could not motivate Natalie to do. Through Maria, Doris was able to get Natalie to *understand* the situation.

How Persuasion Depends on the Way Words Are Understood

"Understanding," here, is not just a matter of understanding the words—of knowing what is said. It is, rather, a matter of accepting the "picture of reality" that the words present. When Doris said "This is easy—you'll learn fast," Natalie understood something quite different; perhaps something like "This will prove to everyone that you are not smart"; or "What you are doing now is too easy —you must work harder, at something much more difficult"; or perhaps even "If you cannot do this new work, you are through here!" But when Maria said almost exactly the same words that Doris had said—"This is easy; you'll learn fast"—they meant something very much like just that, to Natalie. In a very special, important sense, Natalie could *understand* Maria.

Misunderstanding takes many forms; and if you want someone to do *A* and they think you want them to do *B*, the motivation you use may be wasted, or worse.

Noel C., a project supervisor for an engineering department, said "Write me a report on that" to Tim R., a new man who had just told him of a malfunction in a chemical processing system. Tim looked at Noel in amazement, and blurted: "My God— I've got no time for that! I've got to get that thing fixed!" That made Noel think he probably ought to fire Tim.

What Noel *really* meant was, "When you are all through, let me have a note or memo on this, on the regular report form, to put in the Maintenance and Repair file." What Tim *thought* he meant was, "Stop everything, sit down and write a formal report, with historical section, recommendations, estimates and reliability forecast, with six copies, perfectly typed, like you used to do for that consulting firm you were with!" Naturally, Tim resisted such a (supposed) directive, as absurd under the circumstances.

Helping the *Target Individual* to a Better "Picture of Reality"

Many times, a failure to motivate someone can be traced to a misunderstanding. In such cases, the problem is not really how to motivate, but rather how to help the other person understand—to arrive at a common "picture of reality." Sometimes someone else, like another employee on the same level, can do this better than the boss (third party—see above).

The more two people have in common, the better they are likely to understand one another. A boss who understands his people can motivate them more effectively; and the same with a salesman who understands his customers, and parents who understand their children.

2. HOW TO HANDLE PROBLEMS OF PRIDE

Very often people are "hung up" on some attitude or feeling that not only keeps them from doing what *you* want them to do, but sometimes keeps them from doing even what *they* want to do, *themselves*! We call such blocking attitudes pride, or stubbornness, or "ego"; and they are generally based on the kind of "picture" that people have of themselves, and especially of themselves in relation to others.

How to Take Advantage of the Way People Think Well of Themselves

People really like to think of themselves in a certain way, and they resent and resist anything that tends to prevent them from cherishing and preserving that preferred "self-image." We will discuss below some typical examples.

First, there is the employee who insists on a request rather than an order. Very often the resistance is concealed or indirect: *tell* him to do something and he is too busy, or he will get to it later, and has to be reminded; or he will even say, "Why not tell Pete to do it?" or otherwise indicate his unwillingness. But *request* him to do it—"please!"—and you get a very different reaction: grudging, perhaps, but nevertheless compliant. Such an employee likes to think of himself as *not* subject to orders, but as reasonably disposed to grant reasonable requests.

How "Playing a Game" Can Help You to Motivate Some People

Next there is the employee who resents and tends to reject the authority of a superior, but is willing to "grant a favor." This is a more extreme case of the example above. It is typical of the passed-over, unpromoted, resentful employee, especially when older, who hates to be under the supervision and direction of a newly-promoted, younger person.

In some cases the relationship can be saved from a tragic show-down only if the young boss goes along—to some extent —with the fiction that he can only make a suggestion, or ask the older employee to do him a favor, and pretends that he has no authority to require compliance.

Often, in such situations, the superior can motivate the employee to cooperate by playing a kind of "game." If he is tactful, and sensitive to the feelings of the employee—however unrealistic and unreasonable—the difficulty eases. The employee may even come to feel a certain appreciation for the accommodation, and try not to test it too far. He will even be motivated to do his part in the "game" they are playing.

Very often a situation arises where it is necessary to ask employees to pitch in and do work ordinarily done by lower-level employees. Sometimes they are asked to fill in on a job from which they have been promoted, as when their successor is sick or on vacation; and they may resent having to retrogress to a lower position, even if only temporarily. They have eagerly adapted to the new picture of themselves at their new level of attainment; and they do not want to have to think of themselves as back where they were.

Motivating by Pointing to Examples with Special *Standing*

Motivating them to handle these lower-grade chores may require some special handling. A good way to go about it can be to point to examples of members of the upper levels of management who have pitched in to help out at lower-level tasks when circumstances rendered this desirable.

"Did you see Mr. Matthews running that fork truck, the other night, when we were trying to get out that rush order in overtime? He's plant manager, but he doesn't think he's too good to run a fork truck."

"Mr. Leonard has been running the duplicator after five o'clock, when Geraldine had to leave to catch her train. He's the office manager, and he has to stay late on account of it, to clean up his own desk. I wonder if you'd mind helping us out on that. . . ."

"Yes, I know you haven't done any general filing in five years—since they made you Mr. Bowen's secretary. But you do have the experience; you do know how to do it right; and we *are* in a jam. We'd all appreciate it. . . ."

"You've been around here so long, George; you know all the ropes; and you really do have the background to understand how necessary it is that everyone pitch in to get this order out, even if it does involve doing something they haven't done for years—or were never hired to do, like carrying boxes. Look at Mr. Bryant! Now, if *you* set an example, they'll all pitch in. . . ."

How Status Can Affect Motivation

"Status," of course, is one of the really big motivational factors with almost everyone; and when we have worked and striven to gain status, we don't like to give up any of the signs of the status we have won. We are proud of whatever progress we have made; and we don't want to lose it (we even want to gain more); and so we don't want to do anything that even looks like we have lost it.

And some people are very much that way: they won't give up an inch of the signs of status they have managed to gain. And they can be *very* stubborn about it.

How to Motivate People to Risk Losing Their Status

You have to have a very strong argument—one that will have forceful meaning *to them,* to convince them that they should overcome their pride and do what is best for the organization or the group. To do this it is usually necessary to impress them with certain basic ideas, some or all of which must work together to overcome their resistance.

1. What you want them to do really must be done; there is a good reason for it.
2. There are not enough people who do it regularly, or who would be more suitable to do it, available.
3. Other people of higher status than the task calls for will also help out.
4. No status will be lost—it may even be gained—by participating helpfully in an emergency.
5. Real status also involves ideas of loyalty, helpfulness, cooperativeness, and other such constructive attitudes, all of which will be demonstrated by doing what is required.
6. The organization—the group—confers status. When the organization (group) needs help, status should not be an obstacle.
7. No personal feelings that are related to one's position should be allowed to affect the organization (group) adversely.

How Pride Can Help

Pride can have powerful effects on behavior; and often these effects are constructive and valuable. An individual's pride in his workmanship, in his ability, in his achievements, in his contributions—this kind of pride can provide a potent motivation to do his best. Nothing should be done to impair the very proper and desirable sense of gratification that an individual earns by doing his work well.

But pride can have negative effects, too: it can create stubborn obstacles to cooperation; it can cause serious difficulties between individuals who should get along together smoothly; it can generate friction, and magnify quarrels, and stand in the way of harmony. Some of the worst problems of pride occur when people are insecure, or disagree. These are discussed in Sections 3 and 5, below.

3. HOW TO OVERCOME INSECURITY IN OTHERS

A small city child who cannot swim, and who has never been on a float or standing by a poolside before, will almost certainly be afraid to jump into the water for the first time. Yet a month later the same child will be jumping into the water as gaily and freely as the others.

A very real change has taken place in the way the child feels about this experience. The child lacked confidence at first because he had never done it before, and didn't know how well he could handle the problem. He was insecure in the face of this situation, and so did not want to jump.

Unfamiliarity is one of the most common causes of insecurity. People usually resist doing what they have never done before; and can be persuaded to "try it" only if they feel some likelihood that it may be more satisfying than otherwise, or at least, that they will have nothing to regret.

How to Get Someone to "Try Something New"

Motivating someone to "try something new" can be very difficult. Just how difficult will depend on many factors, including the character and personality of the person, what it is they are to try, what the consequences will or can be, what they know about it, the relationship between that person and the one doing the motivating, etc.

On the other hand, some people seem always to be looking for something new to try. It would seem that they must be supremely confident—extremely sure of themselves. But if you examine such situations carefully, you will find that their willingness (or eagerness) to try new things does not extend to "everything," but only to classes of activity where they either have had or would like to have favorable experience.

A typical example is the "meat and potatoes" man, lover of simple American home cooking, on his first trip to Europe. Someone persuades him to taste an exotic dish. He may not like it at all; and then he will be even harder to persuade next time, and even less likely to approve, if persuaded again. But if he does like the taste of the new dish, he will be encouraged to try others; and he may even develop some interest in gourmet food. If so, he may be willing to try all sorts of dishes, but this openness to experiment will be limited: it will not necessarily be extended to every other area of activity. It will apply primarily to that activity where he has had, and has reason to expect, favorable experience. His new-found receptivity to culinary novelty will not be reflected elsewhere; it will probably not do much to change his tastes in television programs, art, books, amusements, friends, or his business activities.

How to Get People to Welcome Changes

It is said that people resist change; that people "like to stick with what they know"; that the familiar is reassuring and the strange inspires doubt. But people welcome change when it is for the better; they will accept something novel once they realize it is superior to what they have known; and the once familiar will be abandoned when the once strange is found to be preferable.

So if you have the problem of motivating someone to do something, or to accept a change, and you meet with their resistance, you probably have the problem of overcoming the insecurity of inexperience. And to overcome this problem you will need to balance "positives" against "negatives" until the change is seen more confidently, as promising more and risking less; and this in terms of whatever experience the individual has had which you can use to help motivate him.

Bridging the Gap Between the Familiar and the Unfamiliar

Arguing or persuading from the familiar and accepted to the untried is sometimes called "bridging"; and it can sometimes overcome the "gap" between the known and the unknown, for the insecure. Here is an example:

"Joe, remember how I got you to try that *ragout bourguignon* in Paris? You know you liked it—you said it was like a very tasty beef stew. Now, I'm asking you to try this. . . and I know you'll like this, too!"

Another helpful factor is the *standing* of the person doing the motivating: if the insecure person has confidence in the other—especially in relation to the specific subject—motivation to try something new can be greatly eased. (Some of the suggestions in Chapter 9, Section 1, are also applicable here).

Leading Others by Example or by Collaboration

A child who hesitates to take medicine can often be led to accept the dosage by seeing someone else take a similar dose. A man or woman reluctant to try a new dance step will be more likely to make the attempt with a partner known to be competent, tolerant, patient and uncritical. In the same way, an employee will more readily try something new for a boss who "knows I always do my best" than for one who is usually rather free with criticism.

Sometimes the motivation problem is eased when the circumstances are less intimidating and more reassuring. If the risk of public failure or embarrassment is removed, the insecure person may be willing to chance a private try. Of course, high enough incentives can often motivate the insecure person to a certain degree of risk; but if they really lack confidence, this is not very likely to be an effective approach, since the unexperienced can be frightening.

The Problem of Adverse Experience, and How to Overcome It

Certainly, not all insecurity is based on inexperience. Much of it is all too painfully based on definitely adverse experience— experience of unsuccess or failure which has brought a conviction of inadequacy, of the inevitability of not measuring up.

Such learned insecurity can be very difficult to overcome, and can be a major challenge to motivation. The principles involved are parallel to those applying when insecurity is based only on unfamiliarity; and the means of overcoming this insecurity are also similar. But the difficulties are likely to be far greater, and the *motivational plan* must be more far-reaching, and the tactics more skillful. Often a strategic plan will be necessary, with appropriate tactics carried out over a period of time, to overcome self-doubt, to bury the vivid image of past failure, to build confidence, and to emphasize the value of related incentives.

It is usually necessary to demonstrate that the situation is *not the same*; that there is some really important difference; or that some significant, effective change has taken place, since the adverse experience, that will make failure less likely and success more certain. Try to convince the individual that the present situation is *different*. Point to the distinctive conditions of the past experience that made it particularly difficult; emphasize the reduction or absence of such conditions now. Stress the knowledge, skill and ability of the individual now against their prior capabilities. Emphasize the factors that now make a different, more satisfying outcome probable.

"Fixing" the Situation to Build a Favorable Experience

Perhaps you can actually "fix" a situation: set it up so that a favorable outcome can be expected. One "win"—one rewarding experience of satisfaction or success—one occasion for winning approbation—can be enormously encouraging. And this can make a tremendous difference in building or restoring confidence and in providing motivation to go ahead and do more and better. One success can do wonders in building confidence.

Sometimes the insecure individual can be influenced by facing him with the long-term consequences of maintaining a negative attitude toward his own capacity to deal with some aspects of life: "Don't you realize that if you never try anything new you'll end up doing the same things all your life?" This may work with persons who are not too insecure, but it can be terribly depressing to those who simply cannot rally the necessary resolution. Hence, it should not be used with really insecure people.

Motivation of the insecure is one way you can greatly benefit other people, build human resources, and demonstrate real leadership ability.

4. HOW TO TAKE CARE OF OTHER PEOPLE'S "ANGLES"

Many a person has an "angle."

By "angle," we mean a special purpose or interest; or a maneuver that may serve a purpose or interest; or, sometimes, a special way of looking at a situation. Thus someone who receives a secret commission for influencing the transactions of others has an angle (perhaps not an honest one). Someone who accomplishes a purpose in an original or special way may also be said to have an angle. And someone who comes up with a new or different idea or insight or point of view also may be said to have "a new angle." But actually, when we say someone has an angle, we usually mean that their real motivation for doing something is not the obvious one.

When we want to motivate a person, we need to know about any angles they may have that can make our job easier or more difficult, or that can affect our purpose in any way. We will need to consider any such angles in our *motivation plan,* in our strategy and in our tactics. Knowing about the angles that people may have can and often should influence our choice of *target individual*. And very often, when we wonder why a person acts or talks or otherwise behaves in a certain way, the answer is: an angle.

If we want to change the way that a person acts, by motivating them to act in a different way, we must first learn or determine *why* they act in the way they do. If we want to introduce a change, we will need to act on the causes of the present patterns; and if we are to motivate a change, we will need to know if there is a motivation for the existing situation, and what it is.

Finding Out about Adverse Motivations

Sometimes, in such cases, there is no conscious or active motivation: it is mainly a matter of habit, and we can work on motivating a change in the habit. But sometimes there is a real motivation at work to make that person behave as he does; and that motivation is working against us. That adverse motivation may be a general one (such as stubbornness, or laziness, or pride, etc.) or it may be a special one that is specifically opposed to the motivation that we want. Such an adverse motivation may arise from an angle.

When a person has a motivation that they know you will not approve, they are likely to conceal it; and many angles are in fact hidden, and are often very difficult to find out. When they are found out, however, they may be ended—some angles can operate only when hidden.

Louella P. was a typist in the foreign department of a large bank. Half the typists got off for lunch at noon, and half at one o'clock. Louella was one of about ten who got off at one. She had a favorite luncheonette quite nearby, the Star; and she always suggested to the girls that they go there for lunch, often rather insisting on it.

For quite a while she was able to persuade some of the girls to accompany her there; but there were more attractive places not too far away, and her insistence on her favorite place soon began to annoy some of the girls. So after a while she was no longer able to lead them there. She soon found that she had the choice of joining the other girls at some other place of *their* choosing, or lunching alone at the place of her choice, which she seldom did.

How Diana G. Discovered Some Angles

One day Diana G., one of the other girls of Louella's group, happened to get off to lunch quite late, all alone; and, because it was close, she went into the Star Luncheonette—the place that was Louella's favorite. It was almost empty at that hour, and the owner served Diana himself. He asked her where she worked, and when she told him, he made her an offer.

"You wanna eat free, you bring in the other girls. Every girl you bring in for lunch, I give you credit—twenty percent of your check. You bring in five girls, you eat free."

It didn't take Diana long, then, to realize that the luncheonette owner was offering her an angle—and that he must have already made the same offer to Louella. And that angle explained why Louella had so persistently urged the girls to patronize that luncheonette. Louella's angle had, of course, motivated her to do this; and it had worked against the efforts of the other girls to motivate her to lunch elsewhere. "And I used to wonder why she liked this place so much," Diana told the other girls, later.

This story illustrates a typical adverse angle: it gave Louella a strong motivation; it worked best when secret; it worked against motivation by others.

What to Do about Adverse Angles

What can be done about such angles?

First, they must be discovered; they must be understood.

Then, they can be destroyed, or—sometimes—they can be incorporated into the motivation the angle was opposing.

As an example, take Louella's case, again. The girls—when told by Diana, at first were resentful, or even angry; they wanted to refuse to go to lunch with Louella; and they wanted to blacklist the Star Luncheonette. But, instead, they made a deal with the owner: they *all* ate there at a 20% saving! They shared the benefit of Louella's angle.

If an angle is dishonest, unethical, or would be embarrassing if known, it can usually be destroyed or negated by bringing it to light. However, it tells something about the motivational orientation of the individual who has or had the angle—and of course this should be borne in mind for the future.

If the angle involves a special advantage, this can sometimes be diverted from the individual who has the angle, to the individuals who have been exploited by the angle, or the organization against which the angle is directed. Thus the girls found a way to make Louella's angle work for them.

What a Purchasing Manager Did about an Angle

Similarly, Chester N., chief purchasing agent for Mogul Chemical Company, found a way that his company could benefit from an angle that had been used against it. He learned that one of his assistants had an angle: he had been accepting valuable gifts from a supplier in return for favoring that supplier with orders. He fired the assistant, and he sent for the representative of the supplier company, which was an important source of necessary materials.

"You don't need to bribe anybody to get legitimate business here," he declared, "and I want you to know that I resent your having done so. However, now I know that you make enough profit on our business so you can afford to give some of it away. After this you won't need to give any of it away; so I'll expect your prices to be, say, 10% lower."

Straightening Out an Angle to Make It Helpful

Sometimes someone else's angle that is not working for your purposes can be switched enough to make its effect favorable. In a certain broad sense, every motivation is an angle, involving something that somebody wants. If you can show others a different or better way to get what they want, or that their angle is unnecessary, it will be dropped or changed to conform with the enlightenment.

Dan H. was supervisor of a section in an auto parts plant. He had an assistant, Nat T., who rode in the same car pool with Dan's boss, Oscar D. Nat badly wanted a promotion; and he really wanted Dan's job. So Nat had an angle: he did as little as he could to make Dan look good; and he took every opportunity to criticize him —especially to Oscar.

Oscar knew that Dan was first-rate, and he saw through Nat's angle easily; but he also realized that Nat might still have good potential for promotion. After conferring with Dan, he called Nat into his office.

"Nat," he told him, "I know you're ambitious; and we're

going to need good men in management around here. But I want to set you straight. We only want men who demonstrate that they can and will support the existing management structure, and who do nothing to undermine it.

"The best thing that could happen to you would be a favorable recommendation from Dan. And *that*, you'll have to earn! And you'll have to earn it from Dan! There are lots of places here that you could go, beside Dan's desk; but if you get a reputation for undercutting your boss, nobody will want you under them. If you really want to move up, you'll have to show how valuable you can be—*to Dan*. After all, it's your job to assist *him*. Now, how about showing us how good you are, at your job?"

Nat understood Oscar very well. His big motivational drive, which had led to his anti-Dan angle, was switched to a more constructive direction—but with the same basic purpose: to get himself ahead, as before. But now, not by damaging Dan, as was his angle, but by winning his support.

Diverting a basic motivation from an angle to a desired direction is an ideal way of dealing with angles and channelling motivation to bring about the results you want.

5. HOW TO HANDLE BITTER DISAGREEMENT

There are many possible causes for disagreement, and some of them are not too difficult to "cure" if one understands the situation, knows what to do, and is able and willing to do it.

We have discussed, at the beginning of this chapter, "How You Can Resolve Misunderstanding"; and, of course, many disagreements are based upon or arise from misunderstandings, and such disagreements may evaporate if and when the misunderstanding is cleared up. On the other hand, there are disagreements so profound that they present great difficulties, and we discuss these later.

In between these two extremes we find a broad panorama of disagreements which are not based simply upon misunderstanding, but which still do not involve serious conflicts of interest, nor basic, emotion-arousing differences on issues that are truly important to both antagonistic sides. Many of these inbetween disagreements can be cured, or if not cured, made less serious or obstructive, by a person who understands motivations, and who wants to eliminate or diminish such a disagreement.

The problem differs, according to whether or not one is personally involved in the disagreement. It is one thing to work as a more-or-less neutral person on a disagreement between two other individuals or parties; but it is quite another thing to try to bring about agreement when one is involved in, and a party to, the disagreement oneself. We have already discussed "How to Slice Up Disagreement to Find Areas of Agreement" (Chap. 7, Section 3), and also "How to Disagree with People and Still Keep Their Loyalty" (Chap. 7, Section 2). There are also other parts of Chapter 7 that apply to these general subject areas. We will now deal with more serious disagreement.

How to Bridge Between the Two Parties to a Disagreement

If you are in-between the disagreeing parties, it is usually wise not to "judge" the disagreement—at least in the early stages of your effort—if you expect to be accepted by both parties as a mediator. If you show that you agree with one of the parties, you can scarcely avoid becoming involved, yourself, in the disagreement. It is best, then, to take the position that you respect and have sympathy for both sides; and that it is important to you that both sides have a relationship that is not negative or destructive in effect.

If it is necessary, for instance, for two people to work together cooperatively, and they are separated by a bitter disagreement, it is probably wisest for you to concentrate on getting them to cooperate satisfactorily in spite of the disagreement. If you can motivate them to accept cooperation as a necessity, this development will in itself have a constructive effect on the disagreement. Most organizations can show plenty of examples of people who disagree strongly about other matters, but who still cooperate effectively on the job. In many cases, such cooperation may be far more important than agreement on the troubled subject.

But, in some situations, the disagreement cannot be sidetracked or glossed over; it is crucial. This can occur, for instance, when the area of disagreement actually involves or affects the basis of cooperation between two fellow workers. In such cases it is probably essential to do something about the disagreement itself, if the two parties are to resume working together cooperatively.

There are several different kinds of courses you can pursue, any one of which may best fit the situation you face.

Bringing the Disagreeing Parties Together

If the parties are "being reasonable," you can bring them together, analyze the disagreement and narrow it down (as in Chapter 7, Section 3) and try to define and limit it. Once this is done, and the results are accepted by both sides, you can work toward an adjustment, a compromise, a temporary arrangement, or some other appropriate arrangement that minimizes the adverse effects and reduces the occasions for friction.

If the parties are so hostile and emotional that it is not feasible to bring them together, then you will have to make a judgment as to what you think is the best answer to the disagreement itself, and try to apply it.

Joe B. and Ethan C. were analysts on a management information systems staff. They were engaged in a crash project that carried top priorities. The work was arranged so that raw data came to Joe, who analyzed it for certain purposes, and who then passed it on to Ethan for further processing; and this produced certain data that top management awaited eagerly.

The trouble arose because Joe had arranged to receive the raw data in the morning in batches that took him all day to work on, so that Ethan did not receive his work until quitting time. Sometimes management pressure was so urgent that Ethan had to stay late, and telephone the awaited data to the Vice-President of Finance that night. This always enraged Ethan; and he blamed Joe, threatening to quit if Joe did not get the work to him earlier in the day. Joe deeply resented Ethan's blaming him, to management, for delays in the data; and he was being very difficult about it all.

Archie L., their supervisor, knew that getting out the data fast was the number-one requirement, and he had to depend on both these men to do it. He sat them down together and tried to get agreement on the specifics of the disagreement, so he could begin to think up a better working arrangement. But the men were so hostile they avoided cooperating with him, and they virtually ignored one another. Archie soon saw he would have to operate more forcefully.

"OK, men," he said. "Here's how it's going to be. I'll arrange to have the Data Section feed the raw data to you, Joe, in smaller batches, twice a day, instead of just one big batch in the morning. You should be able to finish up the A.M. batch by midday. Ethan, you'll have at least half the day's work by midday; so you can finish that, surely, before quitting time. That way, you can't get stuck as badly as you have been. And any time you do have to stay late to get the P.M. batch out at night, you can just stay home all the next morning. Now, that's about the best adjustment of this matter I can think of; and if either of you can suggest a better one, I'm listening. No? OK, then, that's it! Now, let's get back to work!"

Archie's solution was reasonable; and this and his leadership motivated both men to agree to it. An important factor that helped here was that Archie didn't find fault, or tell anyone they were wrong. He stuck to the number one objective—getting the work done. Nobody "lost face"; nobody was put in the wrong. Nobody's pride was hurt. Both men could go ahead with their work, and were motivated to do so.

What to Do When People Will Not Cooperate

There is still another method that can be used when it seems likely that one of the parties will not cooperate effectively, or when you are forced to take sides with one party against the other. You simply place the best qualified substitute in the place of the party that is most easily replaced, or that you believe to be least justified in his position in the disagreement. As the work goes on, then, the problem can usually be worked out, because the party still on the job will probably be eager to demonstrate sweet reasonableness with the new party. After the subject of disagreement has been worked out in this way, you can decide whether or not to put back the original party you replaced, and return the substitute to his regular job.

When this kind of handling of disagreements has taken place a few times, most of the people in the organization are likely to "get the message," and to find ways of avoiding extreme disagreements that may result in their being substituted for, so that the disagreement they incurred can be settled without them.

10

HOW TO WIN SUCCESS WITH
MOTIVATIONAL LEVERAGE

In this world it is truly impossible to succeed unless you motivate others to support your own efforts to get ahead. That is why learning to use Motivational Leverage can be so important to you.

Think of the most outstanding examples of one-man successes. There was Einstein, who could develop the precedent-shattering Theory of Relativity, sitting and thinking all alone in his study—but who had to wait until others (whom he had motivated to do so) tested, checked and then accepted his Theory, before it could become a serious factor in the scientific world. He had to wait a long time.

There was Columbus, who seemed to *know* there was land on the other side of the ocean, but was helpless to find it until he persuaded Ferdinand and Isabella to make his sailing possible; and then he had to motivate his sailors to keep on sailing!

Everybody is basically a loner when it comes to promoting his own, personal interests or ideas—until someone else is motivated to back him. Others may be motivated independently, but most people who really get along well in this world owe much of their success to their ability to motivate others to act in ways that they want them to.

Corporation board chairmen and presidents are selected by boards of directors according to the directors' motivations. Most officers of business organizations owe their selection and promotions to the motivations of their superiors. Salesmen owe their orders to the motivation of customers.

Spouses owe their marriages to the motivations of their mates; and the upbringing and education of children is determined by the motivations of their parents.

The ability to motivate others, and the understanding of motivational principles and techniques can make all the difference in the achievement of specific goals and the attainment of individual ambitions.

This chapter is intended to put the first nine chapters of this book into focus on how they can help *you*, in the winning of *your* objectives.

1. HOW TO WIN IN COMPETITION

Most of us are in competition. Sometimes we are only too well aware of that, but at other times we do not realize it. If you are one of several people in line for a promotion, you are obviously in competition with the others. If you are selling something, you are almost certainly in some degree of competition with other salesmen. And if you want a competition to come out your way, you had better do what you can to motivate, favorably, whoever it is that decides who wins.

But competition goes far beyond such obvious and financially important situations. When you even talk to anyone you are competing with anything—from TV, or other speakers, to sensations or even thoughts—that may distract their attention. And when you are trying to convince—or even to motivate—someone, you are in competition with all their own ideas, habits, beliefs, prejudices, opinions, preferences, prior inclinations, attitudes, likes and dislikes, etc.

All these competitions add up to problems that you must solve if you are to have them go the way you want; and it will always be important to you to know how to handle such situations successfully.

Concentrate on What You Want, and *Sell* It!

To succeed in anything, it is usually necessary to "give it all you've got." You can't afford to be casual about it: you have to bear down hard on it, and focus all the thought and energy and resources that you can on succeeding. And if you don't do that, the people you need to motivate won't believe you really want or need or deserve to win.

But, however vital it is to concentrate on what you want, such concentration alone is almost never enough. That is because the people you need to motivate are almost never motivated just because *you* want something they can help you get. And if you are really in competition, they know that others want the same thing—and probably want it just as much as you do, or more. And you still have to give some solid thought to getting those essential motivations going—for *you*.

You need to motivate them to act as you wish, on a personal basis—because it *is* you; or on a more objective basis—for some other reason that may be a lot more important to them. Either way, you have to *sell* them on the idea that what *you* want to happen, *they* want to happen.

Two Fulcrums for Your Lever

There are two basic strategies for getting what you want. One rests upon you as a person, as a special individual. This is your *standing*. This may work, some of the time, with people who feel a special regard for you.

The other strategy rests upon *their* interests; what *they* want or can gain by moving in your favor. This is your *advantage*. This is usually the most important and most effective strategy. But, of course, the two different strategies are almost impossible to separate; and the best combination of the two is often the winner, and gives you maximum Motivational Leverage.

If you yourself are important to a person in a positive way; if that person has good reasons for considering *you* favorably or for wishing you well; then it is usually easier to motivate that person in your favor. Everybody knows this, and everybody also knows the converse: that if someone dislikes, fears or disapproves of you, it is pretty difficult to get that person to act favorably towards or make favorable decisions about you. And, of course, this elementary truth leads almost everyone to the day-in, day-out, all-directions strategy—or policy—of wanting and trying to be "liked."

No question, it's nice to be popular; and the well-liked person can often move ahead a lot faster. But popular and well-liked people can have their disappointments, too; and a lot of them who depended too much on popularity alone have found that *standing* is not enough.

Many people fail to gain for themselves the full value of *standing* that they could attain, with specific *target individuals*, to reach particular *motivation goals*. The world is full of disappointed people who have been told something like: "Frankly, Tom, I like you better than I like Pete; but this spot calls for a candidate with certain qualifications; and Pete's showed up better than yours. Keep trying; do good work; take those courses; and think about how to qualify at a higher level next time."

If your *target individual* can be motivated as you want him to only by making him like you, then being liked is all the *standing* you need. But if the *target individual* will seriously consider other qualifications, then being liked is clearly not enough *standing*.

The difference—and the principle involved—can be well illustrated by the reactions of a girl to a proposal of marriage. Consider the motivational effects in these examples of girls' answers:

"All I care about is you, my darling, and being married to you. I know we will have problems, but at least we will face them together!" Obviously, here the boy has enough *standing*!

"I *do* love you, dear; but I think we ought to wait and see, don't you? Marriage is supposed to be forever, and I'm not sure we'd always be happy together. Our parents, you know; and we do have different interests; and we don't always like the same things"—etc. Here the boy has enough *standing* to be the favorite candidate; but he still needs some rather important *advantages* to close the gap.

The point is that *standing* and *advantages* work very well together, and help one another. If you have *standing*, any *advantages* will stand out more—they are more readily noted and valued. And if you have *advantages*, they can do a great deal to build your *standing*. The two together can operate with "synergy"—which means that when you put them together they amount to more than just the sum of the two—sometimes a lot more.

How to Make the Most of Your *Standing*

There are "personality boys" who seem to do everything easily; and there are simple, ordinary people who have to work for everything they get. But sooner or later the "personality boys" have to measure up: they have to show that they can actually perform, deliver, and meet the strict requirements of a real, exacting situation. The others, who may be proving day-in and day-out that they can do a job, may need to convince someone that they can also do other things. They can do this more easily if they think seriously about their *advantages*, ahead of time.

If your talent lies in being liked, in making a good impression, in being popular, you should think seriously how much you want to depend on that talent for your *standing*. If you would rather make the most of that talent, and not be so concerned about other *advantages*, then you would be well advised to go in for activities where such *standing* will give you maximum *leverage*. "Personality salesmanship," for instance, can get you a long way in certain products, services and organizations.

Pick a career where being liked—attracting people—is the pay-off capability, and give it all you've got. Pick a spot where that kind of *standing* is all you need, make your *motivation plans* accordingly, and use them on your *motivation targets*. You ought to do well—as long as no one changes the ground-rules on you.

Three Steps to Making the Most of *Standing* and *Advantages*

Let's suppose you have a lot "on the ball" that you haven't had a chance to show. And let's suppose that whomever you want to motivate—your *motivation target*—would probably have some reasons to appreciate some of those hidden potentials of yours. Isn't it only good sense to take these three steps?

1. Recognize or find out what "pluses"—qualities, capacities, attributes, characteristics, abilities, etc. your *motivation target* would approve, admire, appreciate, require, etc.
2. Study yourself, and decide where your "pluses" can fit into the *motivation target's* "pattern of approval." Be serious; be careful; be sure.

3. Figure ways in which you can reveal, show, demonstrate, present, etc. these valued "pluses"—whatever they are —to your *motivation target,* so that he (she) can become aware of them. Try to do this in the most favorable context—a situation that really counts.

What will be the result?

If your pluses are general and broad in their application, so that they meet with approval on principle, you will be adding to your *standing.*

If your pluses have a particular, specific application, so that they fit the very situation about which you want your *motivation target* to act in your favor, then you will be adding to your *advantages.*

Either way, you will be doing yourself some good. By adding to your *standing* you will be improving your chances, generally. By adding to your *advantages* you will be improving your chances for reaching your *motivation goal.*

And by doing both, you will be building still greater Motivational Leverage.

The key to making all this work as well as possible, of course, is to figure out what *kind* of *standing* and *what advantages* will be most influential with your *motivation target.* The more you know about that, the more you can concentrate on building up the Motivational Leverage that will count for the most, to get you what you want.

2. WHAT MOTIVATIONAL LEVERAGE BY YOU CAN DO FOR OTHER PEOPLE

Since motivation affects people's behavior, you can use your ability to motivate people in such a way as to help them greatly. This is truly a sign of the finest kind of leadership. In addition, by helping people, you can gain the most important kind of *standing* with them; and when they come to know that you can help them, and learn to invite your help, you can have a very powerful *advantage* to increase your Motivational Leverage with them.

Spotting the Important Potentials in Others

Everyone is different; and everyone has different capabilities, and degrees of such capabilities. Everyone is capable of doing *something* better than they can do anything else; and if they can concentrate on doing that special something, they will be delivering more and better than they could any other way.

In addition, people who have a particular job to do almost always can do it better than they are doing it. Sometimes all they need is someone to explain to them something about it that they do not fully understand; or to straighten them out on something they have misunderstood or are doing wrong; or to show them a better way; or—sometimes—just to give them a little human warmth, appreciation, or encouragement, or even just an indication of understanding their situation.

How You Can Become More Important by Providing Valuable Help to Others

Some people have what seems to be a knack for spotting such situations as those suggested above, and for doing the right thing about them. They notice when someone is operating at less than their potential—when a suggestion or an idea or a hint or a little added know-how can be really helpful. They can tell when people are worried or discouraged or disheartened; and they are there with the right sympathetic or reassuring word.

Such people make a lot of difference in any group, and in any organization. They are good for morale; they create a better atmosphere. They are usually appreciated and even admired, not only by those they help, but also by those above them, who value their contributions toward a better "psychological climate." Such people usually have great *standing*.

You can be just such a person. What does it take?

Helping Others to See and Seize Their Opportunities

First, you must be truly, sincerely *interested* in other people —in each person as they come to your notice. You must think about *them*—about *their* concerns, interests, reactions, values, feelings. You must "put yourself in their skin"; you must have *empathy* for them; you must really *want* to understand and appreciate how things look *to them*.

Second, you must be *consistent* in this. If you are terrific one day, and really "turn someone on," then you will only cause a bitter disappointment and disillusionment if you fail to be just as perceptive and sympathetic the next time. The others have to feel that it is the *real you* coming through, and that means consistently—every time. You have to be *dependable*. This may not be easy—you have to make up your mind to do it, and keep trying.

Third, you must train yourself to observe carefully; to notice significant indications in the behavior of people. Facial expressions, tones of voices, bodily attitudes (slouch? strain? tenseness? etc.), ways of working, choice of words and phrases—all such things are full of meaning to the person who studies them carefully and tries to learn. Do not react too quickly to what you observe—wait and see. Listen! And—above all—do not react in a *personal* way. Try not to be emotional or to get excited. Keep the interaction on the level of the *other person's* concerns. That way you can *really* build *standing*.

Getting Others to Recognize Their Own Potentials

Very often, people become reconciled to and accept situations that are far less desirable than those they could enjoy. The basic reason for this is that they do not realize their own potentials—what they are really capable of accomplishing. So you see some people who are more-or-less adjusted to jobs that are actually well below the levels at which they should be working.

People often become discouraged, or accept too readily the low evaluations that others put on their capabilities. What they need is to have someone they respect recognize their potentials, and then convince *them* of what they *could* be doing, and perhaps also tell them how to go about doing it. This is one of the most important services you can perform for anyone else; and it can lead to tremendous *standing* with any person for whom you do this.

Learn to think about others, and the situations they are in; and learn to think *for* them. Just doing this can bring all sorts of new strength to your relationship with them; and as they come to realize and to appreciate that you are truly and sincerely *interested in them*, your *standing* with them is bound to grow.

Why Some People Fail to Act in Their Own Best Interests

Often people know what they want, but somehow lack whatever it takes to get up and go after it. Their failure to make the efforts necessary to get what they want may be the result of any combination of such factors as laziness, lack of self-confidence, lack of initiative, insecurity, ignorance of what to do or how to go about it, etc. None of these factors necessarily implies lack of the ability to grasp an opportunity, or to make good on it, once it is grasped. They merely indicate some lack in what it takes to *move* effectively, as required for success.

Very often, a major element in this handicap is simply due to lack of previous experience. Once a person has succeeded in making a move that paid off, they have a greater appreciation of what they can do, and of what is involved in doing it. They have lived through the cause-and-effect of the experience, and so they begin to "know what it is all about." Their effort has been rewarded by success; their "drive" has been "reinforced" (as the psychologists say); they have established a *pattern* of behavior, and this could lead on, and on, and on.

It is something like a baby learning to walk. It needs all the encouragement the family can provide to get the little one to leave those supporting arms and take the first unaided step. But once that barrier of the unfamiliar and the untried has been passed, progress can be rapid.

Inspiring Others to Make the Necessary Efforts to Move Ahead

You can help others to take that first step. *You* can be the one to help them realize—not only what would be good for them to do, but also that they *can* do it—and *should* do it! You can help to get them started. You can use their own motivations to get them to make up their minds to *move*, and to *mean it*!

The person you want to help is your *target individual*. What is good for *him* is your *motivation goal*. Getting him to do what he needs to do is your *target behavior*. You have to develop your Motivational Leverage by building and developing your *standing*, so he has confidence in you and in your advice, and believes and will act on your assurances. You can build your *advantages* by showing him how what you advise has worked for others.

But probably your best *advantage* would come from letting him see how what you are recommending to him has already worked—*for you*! That would amount to proof that your advice is not based only on theory, but on the practical experience of successful application to your own situation.

So, as you develop the ability to motivate people, and use this ability to help others, you will be increasing and expanding that ability, along with your knowledge and experience; and that can be extremely valuable to you when you are making *motivation plans* for your own benefit.

3. HOW MOTIVATING OTHERS CAN DO A GREAT DEAL FOR YOU

In the preceding sections of this chapter we have discussed your being helpful to others in several important ways. Now let us discuss the benefits *to you*—how being helpful to others can build all sorts of values for *your* benefit. After all, many outstanding executives have built their careers on demonstrating how well they could "develop" others.

There are various ways in which you benefit by helping others; and you should know and understand some of them, in order to gain as much as possible from what you do to help other people. And you must learn, understand and accept the precautions that you must take, to keep these valuable benefits from turning sour.

How You Can Learn a Lot with Great Benefit to Yourself

When you think about the problems of others, and work at helping them to solve those problems, you are gaining valuable experience, and you should be able to learn a great deal. Of course, every problem is different. But there are also important similarities; there are general characteristics that various problems have in common. You can learn to note and identify those basic characteristics, so that new problems will no longer seem strange and baffling to you. You can learn the underlying principles that relate to many problems.

If you work on enough problems of other people, then your own problems, as they arise, will not be so difficult or intimidating, because they will have a certain degree of familiarity, and you will understand them better. And also, while every solution is different, solutions do tend to follow certain basic patterns (or combinations of patterns); and so the differences are often mainly in the details.

So the problems of others provide you with the best opportunity to learn about and to understand problems in general, and to gain experience in the development and application of solutions, and in seeing how these actually work out. Nothing could be more valuable to you, when it comes to understanding and solving your own problems.

How You Can Benefit Greatly by Providing Valuable Help to Others

In addition there is another very important advantage for your learning. When people face their own problems and try to solve them, they are usually too close to the situation; too emotionally involved; too "uptight" and tense. They do not note some of the important factors; they may give too much attention to matters that are not really that important.

It is difficult to be *objective* about your own troubles or hopes or desires, and about your own efforts to do something about them. It is a lot easier to be objective about someone else's troubles! And so helping others is the best way to learn how to "see" a problem.

Your experience and learning in thinking about and helping with the problems of others will bring you rich dividends in enlarged recognition and understanding of factors you should consider most carefully, and what to do about them, and how to do it—when you are concerned with solving a problem or attaining a goal of your own. In short, helping others will not only help you to know more about your own best interests, but will also help you to know better, how to go about getting what you want for yourself.

One of the Best Ways to Build *Standing*

Remember that all organizations are made up of people; and the overall effectiveness of an organization is directly related to the effectiveness of the people in it. While some executives rise in organizations because of some special knowledge or ability, others rise because they demonstrate that they are able to help *build* the organization itself—to strengthen it and make it more effective through helping to make the people more effective. In this way they reveal themselves as true leaders.

You can do this by encouraging people to learn, to take courses, to develop themselves, to be better at their jobs, to qualify for promotions. You can do this by counseling and guiding people to fit in better, to work more smoothly with their bosses and others.

Altogether, you can do this by *motivating* others to be or become more valuable to the organization. When you succeed in this, what you are doing is certain to be noticed, approved and appreciated; and in the long run it is bound to work out to your own benefit.

There is no better way to build *standing* for yourself.

How to Be Thought of in a Very Special Way

Once people realize and understand that you can be helpful to them, they begin to think of you in a very special way. This makes them easy for you to influence, because you now have important *standing* with them—the strongest kind, because it is based on their own self-interest.

The most effective way to convince people that you can be helpful to them is to *do* it—*be* helpful to them, even if only in a small way. That will prove two very important facts: that you *can* be helpful, and that you *want* to be helpful.

Being actually helpful to one person also has another very valuable effect on *other* people. Other people know or learn about your helpfulness, and they also begin to "see" you in a different, very special way; as someone who can and perhaps will be helpful to them. Their attitude toward you changes a lot; and you gain great *standing* with them.

The old-time political bosses created their powerful "machines" by doing favors for people. But you don't have to be crooked or venal or use improper influence or dishonest methods, as they so often did. You can act honestly and decently, and be helpful in a way that earns you respect, and trust, and admiration. In a way that will win for you the finest kind of *standing*, and great Motivational Leverage when the time comes to influence someone.

But—do *not* keep reminding people of their obligations to you! People resent this; it makes them feel small and inferior and indebted; and no one likes to feel that way. You would be spoiling the effect that you want to produce; you would lose *standing*.

How You Can Make Helpful Bargains

Of course, you can give some help to some people on the basis of a bargain: "I'll help you, you help me." That can sometimes work out very well for you; and when it does, others will want to make similar bargains with you. It can lead to a kind of mutually helpful arrangement; a kind of partnership.

But don't confuse such a bargain with a situation where the other person thinks you are helping them only out of the goodness of your heart. In such situations, if people find out later that you had selfish reasons, you may lose valuable *standing*.

Some people have built whole systems of mutually beneficial relationships, based on different kinds of agreements or bargains to be helpful to or to support one another in various ways. Such systematic bargaining can be developed by following the principles outlined above.

Getting People to Feel You Can Be Depended On

There is no *standing* more effective than that which you have with someone who feels dependent on you. The powerful leader always has followers who depend on him almost entirely, and then seem "lost" without him.

Such dependency is largely a matter of personality, of strength of character. Many people are weak, insecure and they are really looking for someone stronger, on whom they can lean—someone who will reassure and encourage and support them, and help them to face life or some part of it, or some other person, etc.

If you can inspire in such people the kind of confidence in you that they need, that will give you such *standing* with them that you can influence them in almost any way you like. You can develop great power over them.

But such power carries with it a great responsibility; you *must not* let them down! If they really depend on you, you owe it to them to do the best you can for them. If you fail them in this, you will lose *standing*—not only with them, but with everyone else who knows anything about it. They will consider it a betrayal, and you would lose much more than you could ever gain by letting them down. So if you do encourage people to depend on you, be sure you go through with what you owe them.

Dependability Pays Off in Both Directions—Up and Down

There is, of course, another and much more important kind of depending—the kind that exists when responsibility and trust is conferred *from above*. That kind of dependability is properly sought by everyone who wants to get ahead in this world. And, of course, it also confers an undertaking to be faithful to the obligations accepted. And also, of course, a failure to live up to the obligations will result in great loss of *standing,* while successful fulfillment of the obligations will lead to greater *standing,* and an image of greater dependability.

What it all boils down to is that, if you want to be relied on, you must be reliable!

4. GETTING AHEAD THROUGH MOTIVATIONAL LEVERAGE

If you want to rise upward in an organization, there is no better way than to demonstrate your ability to motivate people. Once it is recognized that you have that ability, all kinds of opportunities open up for you to use it. And every time you apply it successfully, others will know about it—especially those at levels above you who are always looking for signs of management potential, for possible leaders, for individuals who show they can take on and handle the tasks and responsibilities nearer and nearer to the top.

The Wonderful Opportunities that Come with Change

In this world and in this life, there is nothing so certain as change. Everything, really, is changing all the time; but some things change faster than others. Some things may seem to be hardly changing at all, for a long time; and then they change a lot, suddenly, and surprise a lot of people.

Many people always wait for change to be forced on them; they resent it and resist it. But some people see changes coming, and get ready for them. Others even see the need for change, and initiate it themselves.

All this offers the most wonderful opportunity for the person who can motivate others. For a change to take place successfully, the people involved have to change. They have to start doing something different; or they have to start to do whatever they have been doing, differently. If they are reluctant or slow about the change, or resist it, then it is clear that they need motivation. *There* is your big opportunity: show that *you* can motivate people to accept change. Most managers recognize that effecting change is one of their most difficult problems. Show that you can help—and you are *in*.

How you can Use Your Ability to Motivate Others to Win Important Positions

At each stage of your career, from the lowest beginning to the highest level you can possibly attain, you work for, with, or through others; and so you have the natural opportunity to influence them. The conditions at each level, of course, are very different; but the opportunity exists so long as you work for, with, or through others.

Just as some ordinary soldiers rise to corporal, sergeant, and then into the ranks of officers and even become generals, so clerks and production workers, salespersons and employees of service operations are rising up through level after level to superior positions, and sometimes to the top. If you study their careers, you will find that one essential ingredient of their success was always the successful influencing, persuading, motivating of others. And if you have already risen above the level where you started, you should study your own advancements; and you will find that you yourself have already demonstrated—and benefited by—your ability to affect the thinking and the decisions and the actions of others.

Rising from the Beginning

When you begin to work, you are almost always a member of a group—one of several (or many) who are doing the same kind of work. You want to move up—to be recognized by "the boss" as sufficiently different from the others to deserve promotion. What you need is *standing*—something to distinguish you enough from the group, in the eyes of the *target individual,* to give you the *leverage* you need to *motivate* him to pick you out and move you up.

To win that *standing,* it is not enough just to be "different." Many people make that mistake: they do all sorts of things to stand out, to be distinctive, to call attention to themselves, to be noticed. But what really counts is not just a difference, but a difference that fits the *values* of the *target individual.* To gain the *standing* for the Motivational Leverage that will bring about the *target behavior,* you need to be different from the others in ways that he will *approve* and *appreciate.*

Show that you can be depended on for what your boss wants to depend on you for. Learn faster, work better and "smarter"; be on time; concentrate on the task; be *good* at your job, whatever it is; show that you can be trusted to do what you are supposed to do, and to do it well. That way you earn approval and appreciation, because you are meeting the *values* of the *target individual*. It is also usually a good idea not to be too friendly with fellow workers who are not meeting those *values* very well.

There is always the possibility of developing some kind of informal leadership among your fellow workers. Many people try to do this by leading protests and complaints, requests for privileges or reliefs, and so forth. This kind of leadership may lead to popularity among some fellow workers, or even to advancement in a labor union; but it will seldom bring the kind of *standing* with management that confers Motivational Leverage for promotion.

If you have an opportunity to show what you can do above and beyond the requirements of the job, do so; but be careful not to act in such a way as to suggest that you are likely to go off on your own, without checking. Those above you would naturally worry about that.

Bypassing the Jealous Boss

If your boss is looking for people with potential for promotion, following the course outlined above should convince him that you are a candidate, and a good one. But unfortunately, some bosses are insecure—even afraid of being replaced. They are very jealous of any possible rival, and they can impose a serious barrier to your promotion. What would win you valuable *standing* with another boss could win you only suspicion and resentment from a boss who thinks you are trying to steal his job. Such a boss is a good one to *bypass*.

The best strategy here is to pick some other place in the organization where you would be more appreciated, and to develop a *motivation plan* for a transfer. Your boss may be glad to get rid of you if you are a threat. Of course, it may be worthwhile to make a try for your boss's job; but to do this you will have to develop a *motivation plan* that can succeed with *his* boss.

The Four Vital Dimensions of Moving Up

When you get your first promotion into management, it is

usually as a foreman or supervisor. Here it can help you to think of your job as having four dimensions. They are related, of course; but each one calls for different kinds of activity; and each one offers different opportunities for motivating people.

The first dimension is with the people who are doing their work under you. It is up to you to get the work out well, completely and on time; with lowest costs and a minimum of difficulties. It is also up to you to keep "people-trouble" at a minimum, and your workers' behavior satisfactory. Troubles with your people, or unsatisfactory conduct on their part will reflect against you. If you motivate them to do a good job, and to be well adjusted to their jobs, you will be measuring up to a very important dimension of *your* job; and you will be building *standing* where it counts.

The second dimension is the work you do yourself. There are always some things to be done that you cannot delegate. It is up to you to maintain a high standard of accuracy, up-to-date-ness, and completeness in your own work. Those who depend on receiving your work from you will judge you by it; and your *standing* with them will be greatly affected by the way you meet their *values* in this.

The third dimension is in your relations with your boss. He has his own *values* as to how your job should be performed. He will apply his expectations and his standards against your performance—and he will also be judging you by the day-to-day contacts and communications and conferences you have with him. His evaluation of you in your present position, and also as to your potential for promotion, are of first importance to your next step up. You should have a carefully drawn, constantly revised *motivation plan* for him; and you should always remember that you have four dimensions of performance in which to build *standing* with him.

The fourth dimension is with your fellow supervisors—the ones you deal with regularly, and some others; on your level, or higher. These men and women are judging you, and discussing you; and their opinions are picked up by and influence others, including your boss. You work with these men and women; you sit in conferences and meetings with them; you have all sorts of opportunities to build *standing* with them.

Never forget the four dimensions of your job!

5. THE RISING EXECUTIVE: STRATEGIES AND TACTICS FOR MOTIVATIONAL LEVERAGE

As you rise to higher levels in the organization, the Four Basic Dimensions of Moving Up, as outlined above, will continue to apply. But, of course, there will be many changes—not in principle, but in the way they will apply to the different situations you will be facing. Your new conditions will bring to you much greater opportunities; but also the need for new strategies and tactics.

How the Executive on the Way Up Handles His Subordinates

As you come up in the organizational world, remember that your immediate subordinates have also come up. While they are still under you, they have risen above all those who are now below them. This should tell you something important about them: their *values* are different from those who stay down below. These are differences that are now important to you in building *standing* and in gaining Motivational Leverage with them.

You will have some important *standing* to begin with, since you are their boss. But how well do you fit into their individual values? What do they want and expect from you?

The ones that count will want your approval of the way they are doing their jobs. They will want to feel that they are "going somewhere"—moving ahead, learning, qualifying for and being considered for promotion. If you can make them feel that you are not only bossing and using them, but also helping them, you will be building the kind of *standing* that a rising executive should be building with his subordinates.

How the Executive On the Way Up Handles His Own Work

As the manager of a part of the organization, you are responsible for seeing to it that all the work that must be done by your part is done, and done satisfactorily. There is a lot more to be done than you can possibly do by yourself, so you have to delegate a great deal. One true test of a manager is the way he divides the total workload; how much he does or has to do himself; how much he can get others to do—and do well. Sometimes, of course, the division is obvious; but in many situations there is a great deal of scope for managerial ability, one way or the other.

Consider the case of the manager who takes on a tremendous workload himself. He has to work hard, over long hours. He comes in early, eats a hasty lunch, stays late, and often comes in to work on weekends. What kind of *standing* is he creating for himself? What kind of *leverage* will it get him?

Others may admire his energy, his diligence, his willingness to work hard for long hours. But this brings him *standing* as a *worker—NOT* AS A MANAGER. The people under him will be discouraged from expecting added opportunities or enlarged experience, because they know that he takes on himself everything but the most routine, repetitive elements of the total workload. He leaves himself little time to think about and to act as a real manager of his people; so he should not expect much *standing*, with them, as a manager.

Furthermore, his own boss, and others at levels above him, will hardly consider him a promising prospect for managing *more* people. They will be evaluating him *as a manager,* and he will not look very good compared to a competitor who shows that he is really on top of his job by getting so much of the workload handled—and handled well—by his people, that he has the time and the energy to do his planning and organizing and directing and controlling as they should be done.

The executive on the way up knows that his job is *to manage*; and he gains the *standing* he needs to keep moving up by showing that he is a real manager—good enough to manage other managers!

It is true that some managers, in addition to getting work done by others, have a certain amount of work that they are expected to perform themselves, and not to delegate. Here the thing to do is to put yourself in the place of those who will receive and use and evaluate that work. Does it show "management thinking"? Have you put yourself in their place, and made sure that you are giving them what they really want, in a form that shows you know how they want to use it? Be sure the work you deliver to others is as helpful to them as you can make it. That way, they will soon learn to *depend* on you!

How the Executive On the Way Up Relates to His Boss

No matter how high you may go—short of the very top—you will still have a boss; someone to whom you must answer for your

performance in your position. Your *standing* with your boss becomes more critical the higher you go, because, as you rise, there
are fewer opportunities for moving sideways to get under a different
boss.

Always remember that your boss has a job to do. He, too, is
being held to some kind of standard of performance. Even if he is
the top man in the organization, he must answer to the Board of
Directors, and to the stockholders. And even without all that, he
will have his own targets; his own goals and objectives; his own
ideas of what he wants to accomplish and where he wants to go.

He will judge *you* by the way *you* fit into *his* objectives. If you
want real Motivational Leverage with him, you will have to show
him that you are not only pulling your weight on the job, but also
that you are strongly helping him toward his own objectives. Often,
this calls for a great deal of personal subordination; so that individuals near the top, who look to be enviable for their success, are often,
in reality, a lot less free than they were before they were promoted.

Make up your mind if this is what you want; and if it is, then
you must build the kind of *standing* you will need to gain the
leverage you want to use on this vital *target*.

How the Executive On the Way Up Handles His Colleagues

When you are moving up in an organization, the opportunities
you will have to influence or persuade, guide, or lead your colleagues increase tremendously; and the pay-off for the ability to
motivate others becomes great indeed.

You will be involved in one conference after another. Meetings, interviews, staff sessions and get-togethers of every kind will
increasingly fill your days. And the way you participate in them will
almost certainly play a major part in determining your future.

People on the same level with you will be observing you
closely to see how you fit in with their own plans for themselves.
People at levels above you will be evaluating you to determine if
you belong at a higher level. And even people below you will be
making up their minds if you can help them, or if they can pass you,
or how you affect or can affect their futures.

You have a wonderful opportunity to *learn*, by listening and
observing; and you will also be judged by the way you show that
you *are* listening and observing—and *learning*. You have a wonderful opportunity to show what you can contribute, in knowledge,

understanding, objectivity and logic, on any subject under discussion. And you have a wonderful opportunity to offer your ideas, your suggestions, your creative thoughts.

But groups of executives do not just fall down and roll over when someone says something intelligent or shows ability. There are almost always those who doubt; those who question; those who criticize; those who belittle; those who disagree; those who oppose. The executive who gains status among his colleagues is the one who can effectively influence, persuade, "sell," convince, and—yes—motivate the others. Because only when someone succeeds in doing this is the way cleared to a decision, so that action may be taken. And the executive who gains the reputation of leading the way to effective action gains the kind of *standing* that leads straight to the top.

Motivational Leverage at the Top

All the ground rules for motivating others can and must be applied, by the successful executive. But situations at or near the top are extremely complex, often delicate, and constantly changing. The right strategy and the best tactics for them are not easily planned.

The executive who can successfully apply the principles of motivation at the highest levels is the one who has learned how to apply these principles well over the range of levels leading to the top. The man who can sway the Executive Committee or the Board of Directors is the man who learned, long ago, how to persuade his co-workers; how to influence his first boss; how to convince his brother-foremen or his fellow supervisors.

He has learned how to set his *motivation goals*, and pick his *motivation targets*. He has developed skill in making his *motivation plan* to produce the necessary *target behavior* in the *target individuals*. And he has developed skill in building the *standing* to provide the Motivational Leverage needed to make his *motivation plans* successful.

He has learned how to make motivating others pay off—for their benefit, and for his.

He has worked at it, and learned how to make it work for him.

The basic guidelines are in this book. If you follow them well, Motivational Leverage will add something to your life that you can gain in no other way.